Reviving Professional Learning Communities

Strength through Diversity, Conflict, Teamwork, and Structure

Perry Wiseman, Hector Arroyo, and Nicholas Richter

ROWMAN & LITTLEFIELD EDUCATION
A division of
ROWMAN & LITTLEFIELD PUBLISHERS, INC.
Lanham • New York • Toronto • Plymouth, UK

Published by Rowman & Littlefield Education
A division of Rowman & Littlefield Publishers, Inc.
A wholly owned subsidiary of The Rowman & Littlefield Publishing Group, Inc.
4501 Forbes Boulevard, Suite 200, Lanham, Maryland 20706
www.rowman.com

10 Thornbury Road, Plymouth PL6 7PP, United Kingdom

Copyright © 2013 by Perry Wiseman, Hector Arroyo, and Nicholas Richter

All rights reserved. No part of this book may be reproduced in any form or by any electronic or mechanical means, including information storage and retrieval systems, without written permission from the publisher, except by a reviewer who may quote passages in a review.

British Library Cataloguing in Publication Information Available

Library of Congress Cataloging-in-Publication Data

Wiseman, Perry P., author.
Reviving professional learning communities : strength through diversity, conflict, teamwork, and structure / Perry Wiseman, Hector Arroyo, and Nicholas Richter.
pages cm
Includes bibliographical references.
ISBN 978-1-4758-0103-3 (cloth) -- ISBN 978-1-4758-0104-0 (pbk.)
ISBN 978-1-4758-0105-7 (electronic) (print)
1. Professional learning communities--United States. 2. Teachers--In-service training--United States. 3. Teacher-principal relations--United States. I. Arroyo, Hector, 1971- author. II. Richter, Nicholas, 1976- author. III. Title.
LB1731.W49 2013
370.71'1--dc23
2012034791

Contents

List of Figures v
Foreword vii
    Kristine Kiefer Hipp and Jane Bumpers Huffman
Preface ix
Acknowledgments xi

  1   The Interview 1
  2   A Brief History of Professional Learning Communities 9

I: Standpoint 15
  3   A Double-Edged Sword 17
  4   Somber Stances 27
  5   Strategies for Standpoint 33

II: Struggle 47
  6   May Day! Mayday! 49
  7   Stakes and Standpoint 55
  8   Strategies for Struggle 61

III: Solidarity 77
  9   Room Numbers 79
  10   The Four Key Foundations 85
  11   Strategies for Solidarity 95

IV: Structure 109
  12   The Chicken or the Egg? 111
  13   Levels of Professional Learning Community Effectiveness 115
  14   Strategies for Structure 121
  15   The 4S Learning Community Assessment (4S-LCA) 137
  16   You're Hired! 145

Bibliography 147

About the Authors 151

List of Figures

Fig. 1.1	The 4S Approach Framework	5
Fig. 2.1	PLC Word for Word	9
Fig. 2.2	The 4S Approach—Standpoint	16
Fig. 5.1	Eight Strategies for Standpoint	34
Fig. 5.2	The 4S Approach—Struggle	48
Fig. 8.1	Eight Strategies for Struggle	62
Fig. 8.2	Team Development Matrix	65
Fig. 8.3	The 4S Approach—Solidarity	78
Fig. 10.1	The Four Key Foundations	86
Fig. 11.1	Eight Strategies for Solidarity	96
Fig. 11.2	Four Key Foundations Assessment	103
Fig. 11.3	Four Key Foundations Assessment Continued	104
Fig. 11.4	The 4S Approach—Structure	110
Fig. 13.1	Levels of PLC Effectiveness	116
Fig. 14.1	Eight Strategies for Structure	122
Fig. 14.2	Knowledge/Success Matrix	126
Fig. 15.1	The 4S Learning Community Assessment (4S-LCA)	138
Fig. 15.2	S.M.A.R.T. Goal Worksheet	142

Foreword

Kristine Kiefer Hipp and Jane Bumpers Huffman

As educators struggle to define and operationalize professional learning communities (PLCs), the authors provide an organizational approach that identifies critical areas needed to achieve school improvement. In our research and practice together over the past fifteen years, similar to the authors, we view PLCs as school cultures that focus on quality teaching to promote student learning and success—the moral purpose of any educator responsibly serving the students they teach and lead. We also share the authors' frustrations as schools and school systems attempt to implement various conceptions of this slippery term. Without saying, PLCs are hard to implement, and even more difficult to nurture and sustain as cultures of learning.

Building on theoretical models and practical strategies, the authors suggest a unique 4S Approach—explained in detail throughout the book—with real-life examples, strategies, processes, and action steps that school leaders can use and share with staff, parents, and community members to engender advocacy and support.

Moreover, a 4S Learning Community Assessment is introduced and readers are challenged to use this tool to assess perceptions of their schools as to *what is* in order to vision *what can be*. By doing so the authors maintain that school staff will be able to know how they are addressing the four components—*Standpoint* (diversity), *Struggle* (conflict), *Solidarity*, (teamwork), and *Structure* (systems)—as they strive to collaborate in a culture that reflects an authentic professional learning community.

We argue that to equate collaboration alone with PLCs is a faulty notion. What do teachers do when they come together to collaborate? Are collaboration efforts focused on the most important needs of the students based on data? Too often, teachers meet to *collaborate* while having no expectation as to what they are to accomplish, or merely collaborate around meaningless goals and initiatives unrelated to teaching and learning. In Senge's (1990) three views of an organization, we illustrate in our work how organizations are viewed either as (a) not aligned, with no vision; (b) having a vision but lacking alignment; or (c) demonstrating an alignment of efforts to the vision. We would add this occurs through working together, sharing assets, and capitalizing on diversity to achieve what many organizations find as beyond reach. It takes a strong sense of efficacy across the school community to live and accomplish what school members believe: that *all* students can be successful if *all* stakeholders take responsibility—once again, our moral purpose. The authors view this as possible through the four components.

Standpoint: Just imagine if educators faced the complex adaptive issues that exist today by focusing on people's assets rather than their deficits, diversity as abundance rather than scarcity, and the value and dignity of all? Might we be closer to finding common ground and mobilizing efforts to achieve goals that matter?

Struggle: Just imagine if educators viewed problems as our friends, as suggested by Fullan & Miles (1992), acknowledging new and different ways of thinking and feeling, and creating conditions that promote a broad sense of belonging and individual value?

Solidarity: Just imagine if educators collaborated through effective teamwork around issues that mattered to student learning and success, exploring hidden possibilities, finding common ground, and aligning efforts to the vision, needs, and values of the organization?

Structure: Just imagine if educators thought creatively and innovatively to build structures, systems, and partnerships to foster a culture of relationships that focuses unalterably on student learning?

In *Reviving Professional Learning Communities* the authors maintain that capacity springs from the collective wisdom of people and answering a call to action. We couldn't agree more!

Preface

> Professional learning communities are not "meetings to be attended" nor are they "forms to be filled out." Professional learning communities is a term that describes how a group of educators work together to ensure student success.
> —Brooke Carreras, principal, Anaheim, CA

Schools have to rely on their own resources to meet both the academic targets set by No Child Left Behind and the steadily diminishing budgets at their disposal. To that end, many districts and schools have turned to professional learning communities (PLCs). Implementing a PLC is easy and cheap, many of them believe, because the only investment required is in the time it takes to readjust the school's bell schedule, calendar, or room and teaching assignments. This is a common misconception, though not a trivial one.

The truth is that PLCs consist of more than just time and space allocation for educators; they are about establishing, valuing, and maintaining a common school-wide culture of collaboration.

In the early stages of our project, we asked numerous educators around the country (state leaders, superintendents, directors, principals, teachers, and so on) to share their insights and experiences in relation to PLCs. We wanted to obtain their most authentic frontline perceptions, not just snippets of information from the latest publication on the topic. Their responses—in a roundabout sort of way—reflected three possible perspectives, depending on the scenario:

1. We are meeting in our PLCs today.
2. We have PLC meetings every week.
3. Our school is working to become a PLC.

Many educators may have personal familiarity with one or the other perspective, but that does not imply a full understanding of what a PLC really signifies. Does it signify a grade or department-level team? Or perhaps a school-wide team? Does it refer to a specific meeting time and place? Maybe it denotes an overarching school culture.

Although they are not indistinct from each other—they most definitely are not—all three perspectives are cut from the same cloth. So let us straightaway offer a tentative definition of PLC in the broadest possible sense, the big elephant in the room.

A professional learning community refers simply to a school—and its overarching culture and climate—with high-functioning, goal-achieving teams that are working diligently and interdependently to meet the school's goals. This all comes with data-based decision making and an action research approach to improvement. Great, now for the most important question of all: How does one transform subsets of diverse, interacting, and interdependent persons into high-functioning, goal-achieving *teams* throughout the campus?

This is the core issue that has driven our search for a new framework. We have come up with a *4S Approach* by which to represent a new mindset for individuals within the same organization to overcome the twin challenge of diversity and conflict and to cooperate toward a common goal. Working in groups is rarely a rose garden; it can cause frustration, division, and stagnation. The strategies presented in this book recognize, value, and, indeed, celebrate diversity in the school system. They are predicated on the notion that a group may actually benefit from the interpersonal conflict that naturally arises in any organized human activity, let alone organizations as such. The strategies we have devised aim to unite individual members into a whole school culture and formulate processes for improvement—in other words, a PLC—that embrace common goals.

We hope this will contribute to the development and implementation of sounder systems whose norms and criteria individuals can share and adhere to as full members. We happen to believe that the 4S Approach offers the best way to revive PLCs and make them as successful as they were originally envisioned to be. In essence, what we propose is a road map to help schools establish, value, and maintain a school-wide culture of collaboration so that the PLC may thrive.

Acknowledgments

Perry, Hector, and Nick studied this topic from three different perspectives. Though we all attended the University of La Verne, we crossed paths thanks only to Dr. Doug DeVore—our professor, mentor, and friend. Without his guidance perhaps this project would never have seen the light of day.

Thank you Chidanand Hiremath for all your hard work generating the graphics for this book. You really helped us solidify many of our ideas through your designs.

Last, but definitely not least, we wish to also thank all the hardworking, dedicated educators who inspired us to write this book. Working in the trenches can be thankless. Educators contribute countless unpaid hours toward student learning. We have written this book, you are able to read it, and all can discuss it because our teachers have taught us how to do it. One of the most important professions, teaching is too often overlooked; so take a moment to thank your teachers. This book is partly dedicated to all the educators who, like us, work relentlessly to raise the level of student learning in our nation.

ONE
The Interview

> A learning community emphasizes the focus on knowledge; the foundation of which is a culture of common goals and outcomes. Education is a field that is dedicated to continuous learning. Professional learning communities are the "training ground" for this to occur.
> —Linda Kopec, principal, Jacksonville, NC

The big day—the castle in the sky—is finally upon her. This is the moment she's been waiting for. She wouldn't miss it for the world, so she sits in the waiting room, anxious and fidgety. Too restless for comfort, she rises to her feet, gives herself a quick stretch to the right, then to the left. And then, lo and behold, the mysterious door opens and a tall, fit gentleman steps out of the room.

"Are you ready?" he asks her.

Startled, she answers, "Yes!" She draws a deep breath just before following him inside. Her heart races faster and faster, especially as she eyes the Judgment Panel at his sides.

With the introductions behind them, she sits down. The gentleman, obviously the one in charge of this whole infernal process, gives her a brief description of the position, along with the timelines for board approval. Then he reads the first question aloud.

But this young woman is more than prepared. She has spent countless hours studying the district's vision, objectives, and demographics. She responds intelligently to his probing question and to the next, and the one after. Forty minutes into the interview and she's feeling poised. She's on a roll. The panel is so riveted by her responses, so completely taken with her, that they keep nodding up and down in agreement, flashing knowing smiles from ear to ear.

As the interview nears the end, the gentleman moves to throw his final question. A short pause later—*click, clock, click, clock*—the words roll off his tongue. This time his intonation is different. More serious, as if this one was really, *really* the most important question of all:

"Our district is focusing on professional learning communities. Please thoroughly share with us your definition and understanding of the professional learning community, as well as how you would implement this concept," he requests.

MULTIPLE DEFINITIONS

No doubt, many readers will have something to say about PLCs, no matter on which side of the table they may, at some point in their careers, find themselves. How would you respond to this request?

In other words, what is *your* definition and understanding of a PLC? The subject keeps popping up in interviews, staff rooms, school parking lots, boardrooms, you name it. So it's not as if "product recognition" were the problem—everyone is talking about PLCs. The issue, rather, is the pervasive lack of understanding of what PLCs really are or, for that matter, ought to be.

DuFour et al. (2006) argued, "It has been interesting to observe the growing popularity of the term *professional learning community*. In fact, the term has become so commonplace and has been used so ambiguously to describe virtually any loose coupling of individuals who share a common interest in education that it is in danger of losing its meaning" (p. 2). And the longer people struggle with the idea of PLCs and stick everything under the sun with the label the greater their temptation for it to remain on the backburner.

This lack of understanding takes several forms. Some people have stuck to a unique but relatively comprehensive view based partly on their experience, and partly on information gathered from books and articles on PLCs. Most other educators remain unsure how to characterize the "group" or school to which they belong, its activities, or the myriad meetings they have to endure in the name of their respective PLC.

After we conducted a nationwide opinion poll gauging people's thoughts on PLCs, a frustrated teacher from Ohio stated:

> A PLC can be two things. The first way it is often used is as a buzzword that doesn't mean much at all. It's often used like this: A leader at a staff meeting saying, "Teachers should get into their PLCs and talk about the article I put in your mailbox." Or a central office administrator might say, "We'll set up some time that you can meet in PLCs to review the results of the exam results." A teacher might say to another teacher, "Let's use our PLC time to plan the next unit together."

This view is being passed on from district to district and state to state, resulting in far too many plainly confused and discouraged educators. According to that teacher, he later shared that the ideal view should be based on the value of interpersonal relationships, the sharing of best practices and effective strategies, and the tapping of each community member's strengths.

The truth is, as many leading authorities on PLCs confess, the term has been so overused it now borders on cliché. Back in 1997, the Southwest Educational Development Laboratory observed:

> In education circles, the term *learning community* has become commonplace. It is being used to mean any number of things, such as extending classroom practice into the community; bringing community personnel into the school to enhance the curriculum and learning tasks for students; or engaging students, teachers, and administrators simultaneously in learning—to suggest just a few. (p. 1)

Given the confusion regarding the usage of the term *PLC*, our first task is to recapture the meaning, plenary understanding, and spirit of the PLC. This book not only seeks to assist in recapturing the true definition of PLC, but also proposes various strategies to prepare schools to be in a collaborative mode.

Our main objective is to help improve the functioning of any group, team, or school that, in one way or another, associates itself with the PLC paradigm. We pursue this objective within a new framework we call the 4S Approach. This new framework represents the four essential aspects that may be used to characterize every school setting as we move it closer to creating a true PLC environment—namely, Standpoint, Struggle, Solidarity, and Structure.

Reviving Professional Learning Communities is designed to serve as a practical road map with realistic strategies to enable administration, faculty, and staff to meet the constant challenge of building partnerships and working collaboratively. Our framework recognizes that, within the context of a school setting, there is a clear need to recognize staff members' diversity of viewpoints, to acknowledge the natural conflict that accompanies these variegated points of view, and to build effective teams—using the diversity and conflict as a strength rather than a weakness. Ignoring the dynamics of diversity, conflict, and teamwork will cause even the best of systems to clog up quickly as dysfunction will soon set in.

In his article "Schools as Learning Communities," DuFour (2004) highlighted the excuses educators who resist the concept of PLC often toss around. One example is the plea for more direction and training in collaboration with the participants. The common complaint here is that they are usually told how to act inside a PLC before they receive guidance in the proper way to become a PLC in the first place.

In contrast, the 4S Approach offers both direction and guidance on deepening the existing collaboration and teamwork. We believe this is the right approach. One cannot well claim the capacity to ride a bicycle based solely on one's reading knowledge of bicycles and their mechanical principles. More starkly, there is a distinct difference, as Dr. Kristine Hipp has put it in a personal communication, between *knowing* what a swan dive is and *doing* one. Hopefully, by the time our approach is more widely accepted, the excuses for deferring implementation will be nonexistent.

BIRD'S-EYE VIEW OF THE 4S APPROACH

To reiterate, the 4S Approach framework (figure 1.1) does not require a major organizational paradigm shift or even a financial commitment, but only slight alterations in individual and collective attitudes and behaviors. Before discussing the theory behind it and offering illustrative anecdotes to shed needed practical light, let us very briefly introduce the four S quadrants—the "blueprint," as it were. They are *Standpoint, Struggle, Solidarity,* and *Structure*. A successful PLC—assuming one is not just paying lip service to it—requires attention to each of the four S quadrants.

Standpoint

Broadly considered, the school community—whatever its zip code, size, or socioeconomic conditions—contains scores of variegated perspectives and diverse backgrounds maintained by staff, students, and surrounding community members and other stakeholders. Under these conditions, everyone must come together, regardless of their individual opinions, biases, worldviews, spiritualities, to create a successful learning environment and a school with its own unique positive identity.

For any community to shape itself into a cohesive unit, member differences—with respect to strengths, weaknesses, passions—must be respected, supported, even nurtured. True PLC diversity accepts this diversity as a positive attribute, an opportunity for collective growth. This is what makes for the foundational dynamic of PLCs.

Struggle

With all the standpoints in a tug-of-war, the assumption is that conflict is inescapable. This is absolutely true. Struggle is only to be expected, being one of the elements of life in the group, team, or school. How schools (including their teams and members) channel conflict will pretty well determine the overall success of the PLC.

Unfortunately, a common reaction to conflict is to minimize it, sweep it under the rug, or allow personal differences to undermine an equally necessary sense of collegiality. In time, this groupthink—whichever form that takes—will infect the overall effectiveness and imagination of the

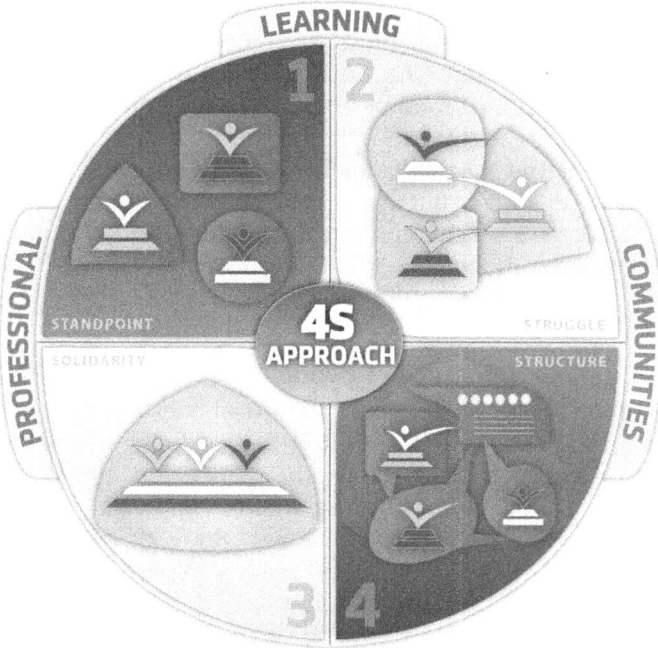

Figure 1.1. The 4S Approach Framework

entire PLC. Other types of environment indicate a greater willingness to tackle conflict head-on and efficiently. This is conducive to school culture and to norms that have the power to integrate each member's ideas and viewpoints into a broader sense of belonging. Successful PLCs use healthy conflict as a necessary vehicle for growth and progress.

Solidarity

Standpoint and Struggle are critical to successful teamwork; Solidarity paves the way to the development of effective teamwork. Should they fail to cultivate joint effort and initiative, PLCs may fall short of their long-term objectives. When the teams are dysfunctional, no amount of collaboration can raise the level of school culture.

Here the communication of research information is key to moving the PLC from theory to practice (Wiseman, 2008; Morr, 2010), but that hinges on the school's ability to make use of solidarity in order to build successful teams. The turning point in the PLC journey is reached only when effective, unified teams flourish throughout the school campus.

Structure

Current and past literature on school systems, resources, and processes have dealt extensively with Structure-related topics. They point to effective systems ranging from tiered interventions and response to intervention (RTI) to the regular allocation of time for professional development to the collective creation and analysis of formative common assessments. Successful schools put into practice effective designs that not only meet the needs of each student, but also simultaneously build synergy with the school community.

PURPOSE OF THE BOOK

The 4S Approach goes beyond the definitional question, "What is PLC?" At some point, the rubber has to meet the road; we believe that every faculty and staff has to at least *begin* the work of reviving collaborative school cultures. Our approach offers a jumping-off point by which to propel schools to higher levels of success. But rather than unseat the wisdom of others, it complements it. The 4S Approach can only improve on the theories on which past initiatives were built in this sector, in particular.

In short, our ultimate purpose is to help raise the level of effectiveness that the educational system presently has in place. But while we have supported our ideas with examples from an *educational* environment, leaders in the private sector, too, should seriously consider the arguments we present. After all, what field, from education to medicine to manufacturing, has not recognized the value of teamwork and united efforts? Our framework supports specific models in almost every area of cooperative or collaborative human activity. Besides, it draws upon theoretical models that businesses themselves have long ago begun to adopt on their own.

Therefore, the 4S Approach and the practical actions it prescribes apply to practically every kind of organization. That said, we do not aim to impose a single, disembodied ideal for everyone. While the general concepts may be applicable to many different organizational settings, the details may look quite different in various settings. Effectiveness, success, and power are nowhere more evident than in the *process itself* that gives rise to and nourishes theory.

ORGANIZATION OF THE BOOK

This book contains sixteen chapters that further delineate the 4S model. Most of the examples are taken from real-life stories so that a balance between the theoretical and the practical is achieved. Chapter 2 provides the reader with an overall view of how PLCs have evolved over the years from its inception to the present, as well as a discussion of pertinent but well-known models.

Chapters 3 through 14 present a systematic examination of the 4S model. Each portion of the model begins with a short introduction, followed by two chapters punctuated with real-life stories, theory, and available research. Each also carries an epigraph from everyday practitioners in the field of education—after all, who is more aware of the obstacles standing before PLC success than school and district employees, educational consultants, and state legislators?

Chapters 5, 8, 11, and 14 offer practical, high-leverage strategies that we believe will assist PLC members in translating each portion of the model into practice as well as assist in finding concrete answers to the perennial question of how to achieve all that. The action strategies are easy to understand and simple to implement right away.

Chapter 15 introduces the PLC survey instrument accompanying the model, called the 4S Professional Learning Community Assessment (4S-PLCA). This new instrument helps practitioners to assess the staff's perceptions regarding all of the thirty-two high-leverage strategies outlined in the 4S Approach.

The last chapter of the book is a call to action as well because we hope that, once knowledge of the 4S Approach has been shared, it will be difficult to defer the implementation of well-defined PLCs within the school context.

TWO
A Brief History of Professional Learning Communities

> A professional learning community is when a group of professionals assemble together to review their practice in a meaningful way. To learn and grow, based on performance data. Challenging one another along the way in a respectful, collegial way.
> —Nkenge A. Bergan, principal, Battle Creek, MI

Since the late 1990s three words have redefined the way schools in America conduct themselves—*professional, learning,* and *community*. Separately, as illustrated in figure 2.1, they carry their own meanings; together they express the intelligence or capacity of organizations for unified action. Which is very fitting, since generally people display more intelligence together than as isolated individuals (Nelson, 2009).

Schools seem to thrive even in chaos, or whatever the external forces at play, if they uphold this semantic/organizational union.

Figure 2.1. PLC Word for Word

A NATION'S CHARGE

The roots of PLCs can be traced back to pivotal moments that saw the birth of a movement advocating "learning for all." In the 1960s, the golden age of education, student underachievement and lack of learning among certain groups troubled many people. Legislators began to focus on ways to remedy the perception that public education was not providing the equitable opportunities it was originally intended to do. In response to the public demand, new laws and policies to help reform schools were enacted. The Elementary and Secondary Education Act of 1965, for one, reflected a new commitment to the improvement of schools. The act established an equitable funding stream to schools called Title I, the purpose being to serve socioeconomically disadvantaged youth (Hord, 1987).

Until then, no comprehensive or systematic path to school improvement was acceptable to everyone. In 1966 a study titled *Equal Education Opportunity* raised awareness of the issue of educational effectiveness by a notch. In a nutshell, it found that schools made little to no difference for students, including at home (DuFour et al., 2005; Fullan, 1991). Though echoing past arguments, this verdict had a profound impact on the public. The passing of the act in 1965 and the publication of the *Equal Education Opportunity* report combined to induce policymakers to promise action on legislation aimed at funding and supporting positive change in schools. Granted, the funding legislation and its aftermath in the 1970s pales in comparison with today's battery of legislation. Still, the studies conducted in the 1960s made a negative enough impression of schools and their effects on students to galvanize the movement for reform.

But those negative views did not capture the whole picture. In fact, they hid an important feature of modern education. Family income level acted as the single most important factor affecting student education, and many educators were bothered by this notion. Among them were classroom teachers who, until then, had believed in the salutary effects of education on students. To them, the new findings appeared to suggest that public education served no tangible purpose. But while some researchers found little or no evidence that education made any difference in the lives of students, another school of thought found a glimmering of credible response to many of education's shortcomings, amazingly, in none other than the *Equal Education Opportunity* study.

They discovered that certain schools had consistently high levels of achievement for all students, regardless of the home income level. In those schools *all* the students performed. They represented instances where school teachers and other adults in positions of authority *did* make a difference. This fact flew in the face of previous interpretations, but it appeared to fit exactly with what many educators had been contemplating for improvement. It was also corroborated by studies in other sectors.

Years later, in an influential book called *The Fifth Discipline* (1990), Senge echoed a similar view with respect to all organizations. It was because of those working within the organization, he argued, that organizations run as they did.

Which returned us to the fundamental question: "So what is happening?"

LEARNING ORGANIZATIONS

The deeper researchers have studied schools showing consistently high achievement levels for all students, the more interesting the features they unearthed and the more affinity they found with a growing body of research in other sectors. Businesses have for years been debating "learning organizations" and achievement-based goals within an increasingly diverse environment that affected decision making, planning, analysis, and other vital processes. The more proactive among them sought to incorporate the philosophy of learning organizations into their daily operations for better results. But while a business run on the model of a learning organization had to focus on results—their "bottom dollar"—schools needed to broaden their outlook if they expected to serve their students better.

Researchers also discovered a strong sense of community among schools that exhibited high achievement for *all* their students, not just for the most promising segments. Their administrations, faculties, and staff had a different attitude toward their "clients," a genuine sense of caring and responsibility for students. Coupled with the philosophy of learning organizations, this sense of community helped create the groundwork for PLCs as we know them today.

DEFINING THE FIVE DIMENSIONS OF PROFESSIONAL LEARNING COMMUNITIES

Researchers have identified commonalities across sectors based on evidence they amassed in an effort to delineate what worked specifically with high-achieving schools. This approach held more promise than one focused simply on what has gone wrong with schools in general.

Hord (1997) first defined *PLC* as "a collegial group of administrators and school staff who are united in their commitment to student learning. They share a vision, work and learn collaboratively, visit and review other classrooms, and participate in decision making." When researchers from the Southwest Educational Development Laboratory looked in their turn at the question of PLCs, they concluded that as "communities of continuous inquiry and improvement," they possessed five dimensions: supportive and shared leadership, shared values and vision, collective learning and application of learning, supportive conditions, and shared practice (Hord, 2004). They defined these dimensions as follows:

- *Shared and supportive leadership* signified the sharing of power and authority in decision making by way of staff input and action.
- *Shared values and vision* meant both the school community's complete focus on learning for all students and continual improvement.
- *Collective learning and application of learning* is about teachers learning collectively and sharing their learning. This component is a key component of the collective inquiry that Hord (2004) had described in her definition of *PLC*.
- *Supportive conditions* within the PLC come in two forms: structural conditions and collegial relationships. Supportive structural conditions contain a variety of elements. One of the most critical components of PLCs includes the allocation of time for staff to meet for collective learning and application. Members of this community innovatively find time within the workday to meet to collaborate. Collegial relationships embrace trust and respect. Interactions between individuals support the work of the school staff.
- *Shared personal practice* is an important element of collective learning, which, if not shared, may end up benefiting only the person who acquires it. PLCs evince real power whenever knowledge is shared, together with any effective practice such learning might entail.

NEXT WAVE OF PLC RESEARCH

With better information available on the positive effects of PLCs, many school districts wanted to make the transition. But how? The above definitions/descriptions enabled subsequent researchers to concentrate on a number of schools identifying themselves as PLCs and to work on blueprints for their school leaders to follow. Despite the educators' rising interest in the PLC concept and the volume of existing information, however, it became apparent that schools needed still more data. In response, educational writers and specialists churned out a plethora of books on the development and implementation of the school PLC model. Their output has proved foundational to the creation of PLCs and their sustainability. Despite the good intentions, unfortunately, the concept of the PLC began to fray not long afterward.

Table 2.1 is a panoramic view of relatively recent positions on PLCs.

Table 2.1. Definitions of PLCs

Researchers	Year	Definition
Westheimer	1998	A group of teachers who are socially interdependent, have common goals, participate in discussions in order to learn, and share certain practices.
DuFour and Eaker	1998	Communities that consist of prearranged teams of teachers who work in collaboration to address specific topics of concern.
Wenger and Snyder	2000	Groups of people informally bound together by shared expertise and passion for a joint enterprise.
Schmoker	2006	The best, most agreed-upon means by which to improve student performance and classroom instruction and hold the promise to succeed where more standard types of professional development has failed.
Huffman and Hipp	2010	Professional educators working collectively and purposefully to create and sustain a culture of learning for all students and adults.

These positions show noticeable differences in thinking. Briefly, the focus of some leading writers on PLCs so far has been on building effective practice through collective learning and professional dialogue. Others still have concentrated on the members themselves.

Despite the differences in approach, the leading minds in education appear generally to be on the same page with respect to PLCs. They recognize their "universal" characteristics. For example, a PLC is not a person, place, or thing, but a process; it is focused on student learning and student outcomes. It is reflective, cyclical, collective, collaborative, and ongoing; and it is effective because the synergy it creates transcends individual effort.

BUT DO PLCS REALLY WORK?

Many people involved in education will reply that implementing PLCs has raised student achievement levels. But is there empirical evidence for this?

To help answer this vexing question, Wiseman and Arroyo (2011) conducted a meta-analytical project to extract, analyze, and triangulate data from thirteen academic dissertations examining whether or not PLCs have a statistically significant relationship with student achievement. The populations they studied consisted of public elementary schools, public high schools, one virtual academy, and a county juvenile court program. These represented a socioeconomically, academically, and ethnically diverse group covering the eastern, southeastern, southwestern, and western United States. Their findings led to the conclusion that with proper practice, PLCs increased achievement. Schools and districts should either continue to build their implementation, or waste not a moment in initiating the process.

Our present goal is to give practitioners well-honed tools with which to put their respective PLCs *properly* into practice. To that end, *Reviving Professional Learning Communities* has enlisted powerful ideas formulated by researchers and reflected in the literature and life experiences of the educators themselves. We address the foundational elements—diversity, conflict, teamwork, and systems (represented by Standpoint, Struggle, Solidarity, and Structure, based on the 4S Approach)—in connection with practical strategies that, in the end, need to rest on a deeper understanding of those concepts than in the past. Hopefully, this will encourage a genuine *revival* of PLCs in schools nationwide.

I

Standpoint

> PLC's allow educators to build relationships while providing everyone the opportunity to share agreed and disagreed prospectives, but still putting our children first. PLCs are where REAL people with REAL ideas come together to benefit our students!
> —S. Robinson, former teacher of seventeen years

Standpoint corresponds to the first of the four quadrants in the new 4S Approach (figure p. I). This component lies at the beginning and constitutes the heart of the PLC progression. Failing to attend to or nurture Standpoint risks rendering all the hard work that had gone into launching and sustaining a PLC completely futile—an absolute dead end.

Although Standpoint represents diversity among school staff, it is important to keep in mind from this point forward that the authors of this book do not mean to suggest diversity of ethnicity or skin color. Diversity also implies individual opinion, personality, experience, and skills. Human beings are as unique as the distinctive print left by their fingertip.

Conversely, imagine if the entire staff shared the same Standpoint, had identical experiences, boasted the same education, and were driven by the same passion. Any effort toward collaboration and teamwork would be meaningless and a waste of time. Their combined intelligence would have the same worth as that of any given member and isolation would rule the roost. This is not how reality works. People are very different from each other and in ways that often surprise us.

With respect to diversity, one ought to simply declare, once and for all: If you can't beat 'em, join 'em. With fear out of the picture, this can be a win-win proposition. Our personal capacity to succeed (whether academically or in our behavior, attendance habits, or any other facet of our educational career) can increase only when we get to know, celebrate, and tap into one another's individual strengths and core skills.

In this part, we explore the reasoning behind the development of Standpoint as a quadrant of the 4S Approach. Chapter 3 ("A Double-Edged Sword") demonstrates why Standpoint is so fundamental to building a PLC and its advantages so numerous. The next chapter ("Somber Stances") deals with the twists and turns that accompany interper-

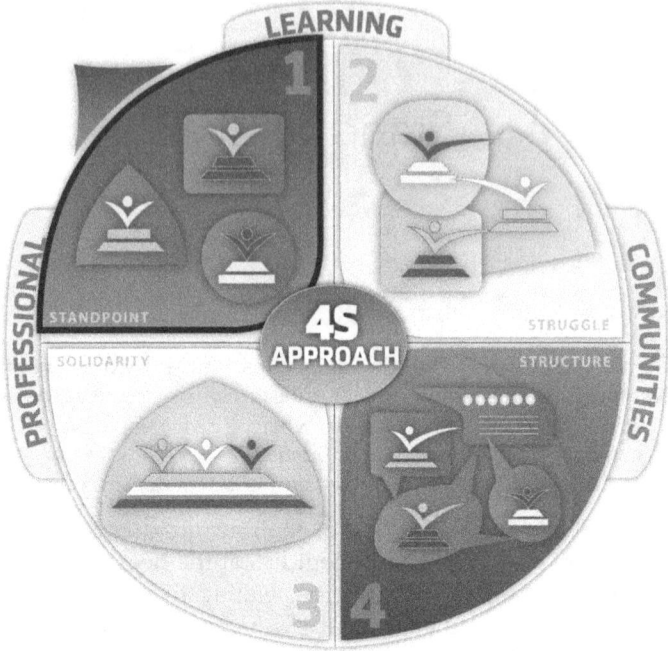

Figure 2.2. The 4S Approach—Standpoint

sonal differences among the members of a learning team. We will share our views of the barriers and embellish them with stories that many people in education surely can relate to. Finally, chapter 5 ("Strategies for Standpoint") presents a comprehensive description of eight practical methods that may help grow Standpoint in your school.

Do you and your staff colleagues view one another as resourceful, capable, and contributing members of the school community? Has the Standpoint of everyone been considered before tackling this or that challenge to improve student learning, the biggest challenge of all?

If so, then you're off to a great start in the PLC journey.

But it's all right if you haven't properly examined the diversity of opinion in your midst as yet, so long as you read on and are prepared to put your shoulder to the wheel.

THREE
A Double-Edged Sword

> For years we looked to outside experts to inform or train us on how to meet the needs of challenging youth when all we needed to do was look in our own backyard.
> —Dr. Nancy Jadallah, principal, Salt Lake City, UT

Standpoint may be defined as "the mental position, attitude, etc., from which a person views and judges things" (Random House, 2001). This may sound like a standard definition valid for all time, but increasingly educators feel the need to refine the existing educational paradigm upon which this key concept rests, to study the diversity of opinions among teachers and principals more closely, and, in fact, to use this diversity to their advantage.

Response to challenge is fundamental to every human endeavor. We need to "respond" not only to make sense of our surroundings, but also to evolve our value, thinking, and behavior. How an institution or organization responds stems from its experience, worldview, and opinions, though. Its "response" may well be as inchoate and imprecise as that of someone marveling at an abstract piece of art after glimpsing a feature of the landscape differently from another.

In short, uniqueness exists at every level of generalization.

But uniqueness can be a funny business. Consider the example of a family used to visiting California's Disneyland Park to experience the "Pirates of the Caribbean" attraction. Apart from repairs and renovations at the site, nothing will keep that family from making its pilgrimage every single year. Yet no matter how many times they board the theme adventure boat and gawk at lackadaisical-looking, inebriated pirates, some new aspect of the ride always seems to enliven their enjoyment even more. It may be nothing more than a trivial silhouette in a window, a never-seen-before scene added to the smoke-and-mirror effects, or the doting chants heard between two pirates glimpsed from the third or fourth seat down.

Remember, this family has been taking the "same" ride for ages, but each time it feels different. Not only does each rider have a unique experience, relative to the broader experience of the group, but also that person feels different from the last time he or she was here.

Standpoint acts in similar respects. It depends largely on where one happens to be seated in the boat, as it were: station in life determines the outlook. Whether we rediscover our favorite theme park, gain new awareness of the selfsame art piece in a museum, or take stock of all the viewpoints inside our school, however, every perspective must contribute in some way to discovering an overarching Standpoint. To be sure, each staff or faculty member has to think about and react to recurring instances of action, inaction, and interaction differently every time, whether one is thinking of a school or a private company. But then the proper question to ask is: How well has this or that distinctive Standpoint fit into the broader scheme of the PLC?

FOUNDATIONAL DYNAMIC

When we say "fit" we do not imply a uniform set of opinions. Imagine what it would look like if all the members of a community tolerated only one opinion? Like peas in a pod, the teachers and principals would have the same strengths and weaknesses. Their opinions and personalities would be impossible to tell apart, and everyone would be bored stiff. What would be the point of a learning community under these circumstances? The "organizational price" would certainly be predictable, limiting the combined intellect of every group or team to roughly that of which any given individual is capable and no higher. Collaboration would be pointless, as would any sharing of skills, strategies, and best practices. Forget any discussion about grading procedures, student behavior, tiered interventions, and common assessments. All would be futile issues that any member could produce in complete isolation from the rest of the members.

But people are not programmed automatons. This is not how reality works. Standpoint implies a unique set of individual skills and passions. They add value to the local community if they are worth sharing. We have adopted this premise as the first of four quadrants in the 4S Approach because, in the experience of PLCs, teachers and administrators must come together to learn from each other's unique Standpoints and, ultimately, to increase the learning of the students—*all* the students.

Collective transcends individual effort when each group member's Standpoint is understood, respected, and valued. Each has to contribute to the group's synergy. This is exactly why the Standpoint forms a quadrant in our 4S. Ignoring the healthy diversity it imparts on the organization can only bring the hard work that has gone into building a culture through patient collaboration to a quick halt.

Simply put, the challenge of student learning today will never be met in a culture that fails its members by ignoring diversity.

A DOUBLE-EDGED SWORD

Standpoint does not exist in a vacuum even within an individual. Belief systems are a crucial component. In *Transforming School Culture* (2009) Muhammad rightly observed that people come to work each day with dissimilar belief systems. While these differences have the potential of creating a bedrock dynamic for the PLC, they can also, according to Muhammad, divide the school staff. In this sense, they constitute a double-edged sword.

This is partly due to the rewards and barriers, not all of which are straightforward. Still, they have to be considered whenever two people convene about system improvements in order to learn what positives and negatives motivate them.

The rest of this chapter will focus on the five advantages of Standpoint (rewards) before we deal with the other edge of the sword (barriers) in the following chapter.

REWARDS OF STANDPOINT

It is too often overlooked to what extent divergent perspectives assist principals and teachers in learning within their school environment. Diversity allows collaboration to flourish, but only if the PLC values each member's Standpoint. Recognizing what others say affords everyone the opportunity to enrich the PLC's learning, taking it to new levels of organizational effectiveness.

Here are five "straightforward" returns schools should expect when they care for, develop, and invest in the Standpoint of one another:

1. Standpoint promotes development.
2. Standpoint brings creativity and innovation to the fore.
3. Standpoint makes the invisible visible.
4. Standpoint breeds commitment.
5. Standpoint improves relationships.

As people work together in partnership toward building a successful PLC, the above "returns" possess key function, some of which may seem rather commonsensical. Nevertheless, they all require a great deal of effort and close attention.

STANDPOINT PROMOTES DEVELOPMENT

The notion that the dissimilarities among school staff promote development and progress flows from our understanding that Standpoint is the foundational dynamic of the PLC process. When decisions are made that may impact the future of hundreds, perhaps thousands of students, every angle has to be considered, every perspective accounted for. This is the way to court greatness, instead of failure.

By way of example, consider a school where the transitions of young students from one period to another created a bottleneck. The bell rings, kids exit the class, and the hallways turn into an amusement park—lots of running around, jostling, and teasing, and basically just not doing the right thing. Although there were plenty of adult supervisors on hand, having to deal with so many students made their task difficult. Clearly there was a problem with the system: too many students were transitioning at the same time.

In response, the vice principal formed a committee of teachers and other staff to tackle this issue. No sooner had they met than ideas began flying left and right, some of them useful, others not so practical, until finally they arrived at a resolution. They found that decreasing the number of students during transitions was the smartest course. One group of teachers would have to release students at a certain hour; another group would escort students to the next class at another hour—cut and dry. The members had approached the problem successfully using their unique Standpoints as a frame of reference, allowing their differences to refine the system.

A few days later the committee met with the whole staff to present the new procedure. They filed into a room, took their seats, and waited for the unveiling. Few bothered commenting. Far from being divisive or self-serving, though, the members' well-thought-out comments would have added value to the new process. But the committee hastily dismissed other opinions and decided simply to move forward.

Here are things to consider when in a similar situation. On the one hand, the committee members' Standpoint held out the promise of raising safety for students on the campus; the system rose to the challenge better than any single mind would have. On the other, the suggestions made by staff members not on the committee were not even considered. How much better developed would the system have been if everyone's suggestions had been debated?

People generally feel more committed, as opposed to passively compliant, when their voices are acknowledged and heard.

STANDPOINT BREEDS COMMITMENT

Not only does Standpoint allow for better decision making and development, as we saw in relation to "Benefit," but it also breeds loyalty and commitment second to none. Soliciting people for their opinions and properly listening to their Standpoints elevate commitment to a much higher level than otherwise possible. This holds true even if the ideas expressed had no chance of being implemented. At least they were listened to—everyone wants to be heard. This approach confers value even upon those whose proposed solution could not be adopted but whose devotion has advanced the search for the right solution.

In education, PLCs rely on members' sense of devotion to doing whatever it takes to improve student learning and prepare students for life after high school. DuFour et al. (*Whatever It Takes*, 2004) consider that nothing less than dedication will achieve the vitality that every school hopes for. But when no one bothers with new ideas, and those ideas that come to the fore are routinely dismissed, everything is bound to slow down—followed by the familiar "I told you so!" Discordant behaviors begin to emerge; staff grows jaded and aloof; isolation sets in. More seriously for the long haul, the members whose ideas were summarily dismissed begin to give up. Such an outcome would be the very antithesis of a PLC.

Take the foregoing scenario and try to picture a better one along the following lines. Imagine meeting with staff to communicate a new procedure. Ignore the input of members and any decision on the matter will produce only resistance from staff and faculty, who view it as just another example of top-down management. They will consider you out of touch with what is really going on. Ignoring the apprehensions will only leave everyone with a bad taste in their mouths. They may abide by the decision, but half-hearted acquiescence cannot replace commitment.

Now consider the same meeting but with the problem presented in all its aspects and with staff and faculty sharing their Standpoints. This would be the scenario that offers the best hope for a possible win-win solution. The system by itself will show a dramatic rise in the level of commitment, regardless of the role played by any single Standpoint. And people will go to great lengths just to move ideas to the stage of action, because debate alone will not make them feel involved in the process. If their point of view is respected and the prospects for collective action are realistic, then everything will change. It's only human nature.

STANDPOINT PUTS FORWARD CREATIVITY AND INNOVATION

Libert and Spector wrote a fascinating book entitled *We Are Smarter Than Me* (2008), where they stressed the importance of seeking and using the viewpoints of others. They contended that doing things in this fashion ultimately builds community and leads to better decision making. Using theoretical modeling and the insights of four thousand interviewees, their study demonstrated that soliciting the input of school employees—in effect, recognizing their Standpoint—produced superior collective wisdom. Every member of the PLC (from the principal to the teachers to the janitors) has to act as a facilitator of pioneering ideas, because everything depends on the creativity and innovativeness of the group as a whole. Clearly, when people are given a chance to talk about ideas dear to their hearts, only the sky seems to be the limit.

And the same dynamic holds no matter where the school is located.

One school in a poverty-stricken, gang-infested neighborhood managed to capture the combined brainpower of its staff once it became clear to all that something dramatic had to happen. Before this moment of truth, neighborhood families had relied on reprimand and punishment, which explains why the rate of suspensions and expulsions in this school was among the highest in the city. The staff responded by coming together to find a way to nurture a school culture that celebrates student success. The staff was not necessarily seeking a stronger student-of-the-month program or adding more awards to the calendar. They were looking for innovative solutions.

Drawing on the Standpoint of each member, together with a selection of unique meeting designs, the school was able to create a school-wide acknowledgment system that celebrated the students' successes—all day, every day. (We will discuss this approach in chapter 14, "Strategies for Structure.") After implementation, negative perceptions started to mutate in short order. Test scores increased dramatically, suspension and expulsion rates dropped, attendance rates rose, families found new enthusiasm, and the students arrived in school excited to put their best foot forward every single day!

This type of intervention requires the knowledge of many minds. No one person—no matter how clever—can create systemic, synergistic change in isolation. Ideas have to develop, but they can do so only when schools learn to acknowledge the Standpoint of group members, confident that "we are smarter than me."

STANDPOINT MAKES THE INVISIBLE VISIBLE

With new school plans in the offing, people find it natural to argue over the impact of any change on their individual and group duties. Moreover, they may be inclined to protect the myopic bubble inside of which they happen to work. That's fine up to a point. However, schools cannot afford endlessly to recreate an environment that threatens to bring the flow of ideas to a halt. Whether or not a Standpoint has the power to influence the outcome, it is still important to preserve a steady flow of fresh perspectives to allow what is not plainly in view to become evident to all in the end.

Picture a principal genuinely uninterested in the Standpoint of others, fearing it might break down the existing system. His school offers students two types of after-school programs, which happen to coincide. The first, which is a site-adopted program, is focusing on interventions for students who fail to meet grade-level standards and has two teachers to coordinate and communicate with other teachers and families, develop the curriculum, and monitor attendance. The second program—let's call it the ABC Program—consists of district-mandated enrichment managed by noncertificated employees from another agency.

Because students can easily shift from one program to the other, depending on their academic needs, these two programs had to support one another. This is important, since the left hand should know what the right hand is doing at any given time. At a weekly meeting with the ABC Program staff, the principal was presented with a new program schedule. He found the change justified. He finally approved it with a thumbs-up and the meeting adjourned—at least that's what the principal thought.

There was one important oversight. Not all the Standpoints had been considered. Some people were not even considered in the decision-making process. Later that day, the coordinators of the site-adopted program who caught wind were visibly upset at the damaging effects the ABC's arrangement could have on their long-established program. Two of them met with the principal to air their grievances and to argue for keeping the ABC's schedule unchanged. But no sooner had they shared their Standpoint than the principal's light bulb shined bright. The invisible was now visible.

Why hadn't their arguments been considered during the planning meeting with the ABC staff in the first place? It was back to the drawing board, this time with the participation of everyone concerned. Another meeting took place with representatives from each program, which helped generate a binding win-win solution.

All too often school administrators think they can transform instructional programs or tweak systems without a proper reading of the Standpoints of those who operate programs and systems. The people in the trenches may have information vital to the outcome. No single person can accomplish this for the whole team or school. This is why successful PLCs must be peopled by operators who constantly seek, invite, and value the Standpoint of others.

STANDPOINT IMPROVES RELATIONSHIPS

This is the last of the five advantages. Paradoxically, diversity of viewpoints helps develop professional and personal relationships. It amounts to a precondition for successful outcomes within the PLC. Where learning and growing are paramount, diversity brings the unique experiences, stories, and worldviews of the members to the fore. Commonalities can only emerge from these differences.

Absent a global Standpoint, everyone would have to share the same strengths, tales, and hobbies, and so on. This would render relationships irrelevant, and getting to know one another would be a waste of time—then, stagnation. Differences in perspective and dialogue are key to restoring healthy relationships, because in reality, getting along with colleagues is win-win for all parties, leading to healthier individuals, teams, and schools.

In the following examples, diverse members' experiences help create positive, healthy relationships.

DEPRESSING NEWS LEADS TO RELATIONSHIP

While sitting in the staff lounge waiting for some copies, Nicole was struggling just to get through the day. Sadly, her husband had been diagnosed with cancer earlier in the week. Although caught at an early stage and treatable, his illness bothered her so much it affected her work with colleagues and students. She became aloof; her mind wandered aimlessly.

A fellow teacher, Ramon, hanging out in the staff lounge, noticed the gloom on her face and asked her what was wrong. Before uttering a word, she broke down. He quickly grabbed some tissue for her and listened. She told him everything.

How ironic, he thought. A few years back he had received a similar diagnosis, sought treatment, and has never felt healthier in his life.

Over the next few weeks they met in the staff lounge—same time, same place. He shared with her his experience fighting for his health, offering his insights. Their families occasionally had dinner together, providing a great support system. His insights led to hope. Now, instead of coming to work miserable and depressed each day, and looking like a lifeless drone, Nicole came with faith and optimism.

She realized her willingness to disclose, appear vulnerable, and share experiences led to this encouraging development. Not only that, but also their differences, which drove them to share thoughts about changing one's life around. The result was that, through thick and thin, Nicole and Ramon were close confidants as well as colleagues.

ONE STRATEGY SPARKS ANOTHER . . . AND ANOTHER

Poised and excited, John walked out of the principal's office. He was selected to pilot the student responder system in his classroom. The student responder system was a great way to conduct a quick poll to measure student comprehension of a particular lesson. The results would be immediately available.

There was only one problem. While he had always been open to new strategies, technology was not his strongest suit. His real forte was curriculum, engagement, and management strategies. He went back to his classroom and tinkered with the new hardware. After about an hour or so of absolute frustration, he called it a day, packed his things, and headed home.

The next morning, before school started, he stood in the hallway talking to a few colleagues about his new endeavor. A first-year teacher, Barbara, who was still getting her feet wet with classroom management, walked by and overheard the group hobnobbing about technology, which happened to be her passion. She could figure out any novel software with or without direction. So she chimed in, "What are you guys talking about?" It was a little out of character. Barbara was normally shy and timid, but not when it came to technology.

When John found out about her credential-program focus on classroom technology and her familiarity with the student responder system, they both decided to meet for a half-hour in his classroom after school.

Their "quick" meeting stretched into a three-hour *sharing* marathon. The responders were set up, ready for the next day, and he got to know the ins and outs. He inquired about technology as much as he could; she asked about classroom management, specifically how to get the tougher students to participate in classroom activities. Their assets complemented each other. The surprising thing was that, previous to this meeting, they used to greet each other with only a polite "hello" in passing. They rarely crossed paths and shared no students; they didn't even teach the same subject. And here they were getting together every week without fail to share instructional strategies and practices.

A simple chitchat about technology had led to a healthy relationship, and now two colleagues are assisting one another. This is the absolute best.

As teachers we spend a lot of time together in the workplace, often without noticing each other. Take advantage of that time. Value the Standpoint of others. Find ways to connect. Build trusting relationships.

FOUR

Somber Stances

> Egos and pet projects must be thrown aside, along with any pompous notions such as seniority or tenure. Honest and exposed, the truth and proof of how and when and why students are mastering content must be laid bare without emotion.
>
> —Kathy Baker, principal, Post Falls, ID

There is no reason why incentives should not cohere with the Standpoint, if they help move the PLC journey forward. But this is a tough business. There are at least two sides to every issue, and any hurdles that arise are simply the natural consequence of diverse experience, education, opinion, and so forth.

The four sticking points relating to Standpoint are

1. Standpoint can damage relationships.
2. Nurturing Standpoint takes time.
3. Position affects on Standpoint.
4. Standpoint constantly changes.

Their main characteristics are observable in the following simple "Somber Stances" story.

On a typical Monday morning the front office comes alive with foot traffic. The school day will begin shortly, as parents drop off forgotten items for their kids and ask about upcoming activities. Meanwhile, the phones are ringing off the hook, as usual. Behind closed doors, Principal Matthew confers with an angry parent disputing her child's involvement in a recent problem involving discipline. Despite all the hustle and bustle, this seems pretty well like any other day.

Matthew's door then opens. The parent thanks him for his time and Matthew quickly heads outside for morning supervision. On his way he notices three staff members whispering together with a front-office clerk.

He overhears two names: Julie and Kelly. No big deal, he thinks, and moves on. Fifteen minutes later the bell rings. Students rush to class enthusiastically. With no pressing business, he decides to resume his other morning tasks—meetings, classroom walkthroughs, and such. Before that he steps back into his office. The very moment he does, his secretary informs him about a scuffle between the two teachers.

Ah-ha, he thinks, that explains the early morning gossip. The altercation, he learns, had gotten pretty heated. Julie and Kelly had been tossing patronizing remarks at each other, raising their voices, rolling their eyes, and now they were ignoring one another. However important the issue between them, this morning's failure in decorum was witnessed by an astonished parent, students, not to mention a few peers. It's a shame, because they are teammates.

STANDPOINT CAN DAMAGE RELATIONSHIPS

Although Standpoint enhances interpersonal relationships, as we saw in the last chapter, it also has the potential to damage those relationships with the blink of an eye. Trust is on the line every moment that personal differences and circumstances are disregarded or denied their constructive value. As Ryan (2003) argued in *The Power of Patience*,

> In the course of going about our business—at work, at home, at the grocery store, at community functions and private dinner parties—we bump against people every day. And lo and behold—they're different from us. Not in the ways that their brains take information. They also have different priorities, motivations, histories, and cultures. We all know this in theory and in the name of tolerance, we say it's good. But in fact, many of us don't really believe it. Consequently, we spend a great deal of energy trying to get the rest of the world to behave as we believe they should. (pp. 39–40)

Ryan adds that patience and empathy for others can bring success, even if personal Standpoints are under constant scrutiny. Like Julie and Kelly, however, some people flat out refuse to give in to others. Perhaps they fail to fathom the toll such an attitude can take on the organization as a whole. They end up hurting PLC efforts because meager relations are the very antithesis of teamwork, partnership, and collaboration. Poor relationships impede the flow of ideas and commitment; once groupthink sets in, they always lead to poor decision making. While it may be socially tolerable to disagree, Standpoint cannot be allowed to go south at the slightest hint of conflict.

Why are Julie and Kelly so reluctant to work out their issue in calm fashion? Matthew complains to his secretary. He promptly clears his calendar for a meeting with them. This will take time to fix, but unbridled conflict is never an alternative. His school has to behave like a learning community. Surely, a healthy PLC does not allow tensions to fester, with all the stress, rumor-mongering, and tittle-tattle that this implies. Any other person in his place probably would have picked sides, closing any room for a sense of togetherness, teamwork, and collaboration.

NURTURING STANDPOINT TAKES TIME

In connection with Standpoint, there are two identifiable ways in which to conduct business over time. One, people can ignore or dispute each other's stances to the point of preemptively throwing the value of differing viewpoints into doubt. They may prefer, in Ryan's words, "[to] spend a great deal of energy trying to get the rest of the world to behave as we believe they should." This approach takes different forms—perhaps a principal refusing to listen to the input of faculty or staff before coming to a decision, or a teacher belittling the stances or beliefs of colleagues; it may happen some of the time or it may be endemic. Whatever the case, messy relationships need time to change.

Two, some people may take genuine interest in the feelings, attitudes, and ideas of others. This is the best way to ensure the health of the PLC. However, they must spend the proper time to engage staff, encouraging them to talk, value new ideas, and work out differences—a lot of time! But who ever said that cultivating Standpoint would be quick and easy? It can prove to be a messy, nonlinear process requiring a great deal of commitment.

That is the choice. Principals and teachers in PLCs should either spend their precious time wisely to speak to the value of diversity in Standpoints in their school or just fritter away their time, resting content on unproductive arguments, personal drama, and bad relations.

In the end Matthew sat down with the two bickering teachers. After hearing them out individually, he realized that the whole squabble revolved around a simple misunderstanding. That, at least, was his impression. Julie had been strapped for time that morning, so she used a copy machine in the front office, which normally was off-limits to teachers. She claimed she had intended to ask Matthew first, but he had been meeting with a parent at the time. When Kelly—who was on a second career and had just begun teaching this year—noticed Julie's relatively trivial violation, she jokingly called her colleague to the carpet.

"Didn't you get the memo about the copy machine last week?" Kelly had teased her colleague. That opening volley caused their conversation to spiral out of control. Yet shouting and sneering at each other betrayed an attitude wholly disproportional to the actual "dispute," if one could call it that. Later, inside the principal's office, Kelly insisted her initial comment was nothing more than friendly teasing. Whatever the intent, Julie took it as patronizing and rude.

Finally, Julie had blurted out in frustration to the principal, "How dare she try and scold me. I deserve more respect than that. And Kelly is just a first-year teacher too!"

Her defense almost causes Matthew to fall out of his chair, but he does not want to look fazed in front of them. Besides, if he rushed to judgment now, he might appear to take sides, which would only worsen the situation. Instead, he acknowledges Julie's Standpoint, the one that led to Kelly's remark in the first place.

POSITION CAN HAVE AN EFFECT ON STANDPOINT

Organizational position can impact the Standpoint of any individual holding that position. It may take the form of a principal who feels entitled to use his authority to influence others. Or perhaps an isolated classroom teacher seeks to persuade others of his or her myopic view of a particular situation. Or another member expects certain privileges because of seniority or tenure.

In his book *Seeing Systems*, Oshry (2007) argued that no matter what a person's position happens to be in the organization—top, middle, or bottom—distinct dynamics will emerge to impact perceptions. He claimed, "Tops feel *burdened* by unmanageable complexity. Bottoms feel *oppressed* by insensitive higher-ups. Middles feel *torn*—they become weak, confused, fractionated, with no minds of their own" (p. 64). This points to the often perplexing web of interactions, relationships, and behaviors that make life in any organization tough. That said, different positions yield different experiences; different lenses yield different perceptions. Whether or not an organizational chart exists, schools and districts align themselves top down, not diagonally across the same plane.

This barrier merits careful consideration. But let's continue with our story.

No sooner had Julie's comment left her lips than Matthew noticed Kelly "closing up." She crosses her arms and assumes a posture facing away from Julie. She is clearly disappointed, and Matthew thinks, "This conversation isn't going as planned." Julie's first comment had visibly upset Kelly, who in turn brings up—completely out of the blue—an old issue that had supposedly been resolved months ago. Julie happened to be the teacher of Kelly's son, whom she had apparently given a B+ on his semester report card. Kelly wasn't too happy about this grade and felt he deserved an A.

Obviously, failing to deal properly with a grading issue in the past got in the way of progress and mutual trust. But that old issue served, in the end, to shed a new light on this morning's altercation, and Matthew's Standpoint shifted again at the drop of a dime. The invisible was now visible.

STANDPOINT CAN CONSTANTLY CHANGE

People's viewpoints are constantly being shaped, reshaped, and bent out of shape. To an objective observer, not to speak of discerning actors, it may seem like a moving target. With so many factors to consider, hearsay alone can spark off a conflict, and new current opinions, or the presence of a larger group at the meeting, might alter individual perspectives.

In *Creative Whack Pack*, von Oech (2006) offered this piece of advice for the discovery of new ideas in any field. "Finding new ideas is like prospecting for gold," he wrote. "If you look in the same old places, you'll find tapped out veins. But if you venture off the beaten path, you'll improve your chances of discovering new ideas." The discerning actor in any group situation will carry out his or her tasks with others in hopes of drawing inspiration from them. The only caveat is that the exploration made possible by listening, patience, and empathy must somehow steer individual and collective Standpoints in the right direction. To achieve this, members have to be able and willing to challenge one another by asking, among other questions, "Why are we here?" It's an exhaustive process, to be sure, but change takes a great deal of time and effort to bring to fruition.

Now that Julie and Kelly's underlying issue has come out in the open, Matthew arrives at a better understanding of the breakdown in their relationship. It won't be easy finding common ground, so he employs timely advice to guide their conversation:

- Remaining calm at all times.
- Using good listening skills (e.g., mirroring, paraphrasing, and acknowledging).
- Making sure that neither party dominates the conversation.
- Remaining neutral.
- Helping both to avoid entrenched positions by exploring underlying interests and needs.
- Pointing out the effect the conflict has on performance, others, and the school.
- Taking time to summarize.

After about an hour of intense but relatively healthy dialogue, the teachers begin to appreciate more each other's positions. Apologies are offered and accepted, agreements reached, and their respective Standpoints openly acknowledged. It's a great accomplishment! Thanks to Matthew's timely intervention, openness and honesty all around will grow their relationship. He knows well, from the moment he got wind of the confrontation, that turning a blind eye on a squabble like that would not postpone his intervention for long. So he acts quickly, his own Standpoint being that success comes when principals and teachers collaborate and work together regardless of the circumstances. Short of that, the students would have to suffer the consequences sooner or later.

NOW WHAT?

How should people work together under the duress of battle-hardened perspectives?

The dispute between Julie and Kelly reveals only a speck of the interaction that routinely takes place inside a PLC. What about all the other conversations and dealings? Are they helping or hurting your collaborative efforts? Does everyone in your school listen to and honestly try to understand each other's Standpoint? Are both rewards and barriers appreciated enough in your school? Which one is considered more important?

With accountability pressing for change and budget cuts deeper than ever, principals and teachers have no choice but to work smarter, not harder. Dismissing the advantages of Standpoint will only alienate members, waste resources, and, basically, just spin the wheel.

In the next chapter, "Strategies for Standpoint," we will examine practical strategies that help administration, faculty, and staff keep the barriers in check. When the eight strategies are embedded in a school culture, becoming "the way we do business around here," diversity and Standpoint can build up into a force for solid development, creativity, commitment, and interpersonal relationships. That's what the PLC is all about.

FIVE
Strategies for Standpoint

> It takes a village [professional learning communities] to strategically mold a child for academic success.
> —Myron Cortez-Cornich, principal, Wilmington, DE

We need to get the nuts and bolts straight. This chapter presents eight practical strategies (figure 5.1) aimed at strengthening diversity in the PLC and short of which one will find only frustration and constant spinning of wheels. The active members of a PLC must

1. Build relationships and trust by extending your own trust.
2. Discover and solicit the strengths of others and strategically assign staff.
3. Use effective meeting designs and seek regular input, both formal and informal.
4. Take the time to walk in others' shoes.
5. Celebrate diversity often.
6. Reflect on your own perspectives and how others may react.
7. Strengthen union and administration relationships.
8. Learn the historical and political history of the school and community.

Human nature is, in part, biologically wired for the "negative." Long ago, we learned to be wary of strangers and unknown dangers; we do everything to protect ourselves from them. Meeting someone for the first time brings out our mental antennas; we tend to search for telltale signs that confirm our worst fears, and then approach the stranger with the utmost caution.

Trust, on the other hand, implies feelings of reassurance despite limited information or evidence. However limited at first, though, information tends to grow over time to become more reliable and perhaps even

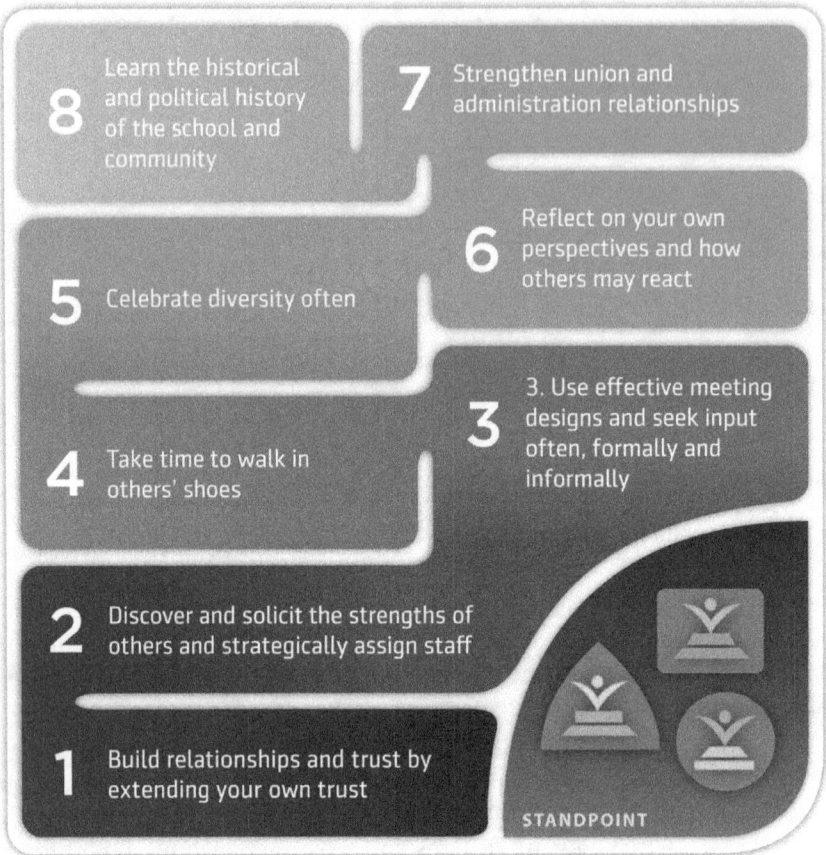

Figure 5.1. Eight Strategies for Standpoint

conclusive. In public education, relationships and trust are expected to develop with a few quick introductions during "ice-breaking" activities at the beginning of each school year. It is crucial, therefore, that members work in earnest to incorporate Standpoint in their day-to-day dealings.

STRATEGY 1: BUILD RELATIONSHIPS AND TRUST BY EXTENDING YOUR OWN TRUST

This strategy allows members to be proactive, rather than reactive, in their dealing with one another. Writer and educator Neal Maxwell once said, "It's better to trust and sometimes be disappointed than to be forever mistrusting and be right occasionally."

Rather than demand that other members demonstrate their worthiness and that their trust be earned, we should extend our trust to show how much we believe in them. Interpersonal relationships should reflect our acceptance of other people's honesty and our lack of fear of the dreaded "hidden agenda." By taking the initiative, we equally allow trust to be reciprocated. Without a doubt, this improves the prospect of agreement in the future.

Below are four actions to guide the practice of Extending Trust, with a view to strengthening member relationships and, by extension, the PLC.

Action 1: Whether in a large group meeting or private one-on-one discussion, be sure to regard everything other members say as authentic. Listen carefully and accurately; speak to them clearly and honestly. Furthermore, be clear about your own intentions. Once other members feel confident with your open-mindedness and willingness in principle to accept their views, they will react in kind. Mutual trust makes for solid foundations.

Action 2: Be sure to demonstrate your faith that other members will deliver on any promises they make. When a member makes you a promise, give him or her the benefit of the doubt. Others members will note by association your readiness to trust their personal and professional judgments, as well; and they will extend the same measure of trust to you.

Action 3: Demonstrate your trust by sharing information with PLC members—stifled communication only breeds mistrust. Information sharing does not mean that one ought to gossip or divulge personal information about coworkers as a matter of policy. It does mean open and free sharing on important issues. Granted, there are risks to sharing information. It must be done wisely and always with the aim of building trusting relationships. The idea here is to have better, more inclusive communication.

Action 4: Remember that PLC members are human and that human beings make many mistakes. But mistakes are unavoidable, not simply unintentional, so there is no need to make them into something they are not. Don't let a bad experience keep you from trusting colleagues. Give them the benefit of the doubt; let them demonstrate their willingness not to repeat their mistakes. That is not to say that trust will solidify your relationships overnight. It takes time to incorporate Standpoint into a PLC. Being mindful of your own actions and *how* you express trust in practice will foster feelings of satisfaction among the members and make them more productive. Everyone wins when the work is carried out in a trusting and cooperative atmosphere.

STANDPOINT STRATEGY 2: DISCOVER AND SOLICIT THE STRENGTHS OF OTHERS AND STRATEGICALLY ASSIGN STAFF

While working on a complex research project, a group of students gathered around the teacher in charge. The teacher, being familiar with the project, explained that after dissecting the project into three separate but equally important tasks she determined that successful completion of the project demanded good math skills (for measuring quantitative data), good interpersonal skills (for conducting focus-group interviews), and good writing skills (for properly reporting the data and findings). She gave the students an opportunity to express their familiarity and level of comfort with each of these three tasks. During the process the strengths of the students came to light and tasks were assigned. The research project proved a success because every student was able to contribute his or her unique skills.

Discovering and soliciting the strengths of others and strategically assigning staff is a strategy for the recognition, valuation, and use of Standpoint to the PLC's advantage. As American actress and author Marilu Henner said: "Everyone thrives most in his or her own unique environment." Accordingly, each member can contribute differently to the team. Thanks to open assessment and the incorporation of member Standpoints, diversity of experience and of expertise has to be recognized and utilized to the PLC's benefit. This is the strategy that will allow your PLC to work smartly, efficiently, and successfully.

Here are some actions to guide effort at strengthening your PLC via the strategic assignment of staff.

Action 1: To put it simply, *ask*! By surveying the members for their experiences and expertise, you may discover a wealth of knowledge and a diversity of skills, talents, and other available resources. This action will help you identify Standpoint strengths for each task. Building strong relationships requires this level of genuine interest in colleagues.

Action 2: Encourage staff members to visit classrooms. Nonjudgmentally looking in on one another's classrooms may improve expertise, classroom management skills, teaching styles, and even decorating tastes. Informal visits promote interaction and conversation among members, and hopefully lead to more discoveries.

Action 3: To complete a project or attain a goal, needs and roles must be properly defined. Doing so is conducive to the creation of a road map that everyone can follow. A clear examination of organizational needs and goals allows the PLC to maximize each member's contributions to the overall effort. Combined with adequate knowledge of the strengths of the members, this should give their talents a strategic role to play in the outcome.

Action 4: Remember that schools do not operate in a vacuum; therefore, it is necessary to cast a wide net when soliciting other people's strengths. Schools have to expand the reach of their PLC in order both to motivate and to involve the community. Nor is the wider "community" restricted to parents; it may include local businesses, legislators, and higher education institutions. Expanding the pool of member strengths makes the assignment of tasks much easier. It simply makes strategic sense.

In sum, the purpose of the second strategy—discovering and soliciting the strengths of others and strategically assigning staff—is to match member Standpoint with necessary tasks. This can seem like trying to fit the pieces of a puzzle together; like any good puzzle it takes time to figure out where the pieces go. Some pieces appear to match, when in fact they do not. A correct match will give the PLC a value greater than the sum of its parts.

STANDPOINT STRATEGY 3: USE EFFECTIVE MEETING DESIGNS AND SEEK REGULAR INPUT, BOTH FORMAL AND INFORMAL

People want to be heard. They pine for the opportunity to share their personal Standpoints, opinions, and ideas. Sharing wakens their creativity and innovative senses, and renders the invisible visible. But it carries all sorts of benefits. All in all, people are more inclined to commit at higher levels and to let their relationships mature. This can happen in a variety of venues, from a casual conversation in the staff lounge to the formal setting of a staff meeting.

This strategy actively seeks to place input relating to Standpoint at the advantage of the PLC. According to Elle Macpherson, an Australian model, actress, and businesswoman, "For me, just being on the cover of a magazine wasn't enough. I began to think, what value is there in doing something in which you have no creative input?" It was this Standpoint that prompted her finally to leave the modeling world and go into business for herself. Surface involvement had failed to satisfy her. By the same token, to obtain its members' commitment to innovation and change a PLC must help them recognize the value in what they are doing.

Are the typical staff meetings at your school or district nothing more than gatherings, where up-to-date information flows in one direction, top down? Do they run, as Delisio (2009) put it, on the pattern of "read the news and run," much like a press briefing? Or are they facilitated by clear objectives, generating the best solutions on the most difficult problems?

Here are three straightforward actions that principals and teachers can adopt to facilitate their meetings within a PLC framework.

Action 1: It is essential to familiarize those responsible for conducting or facilitating meetings (team leaders, principals, department chairs, etc.) with a variety of possible meeting designs whose goal is to engage the members in a focused, meaningful dialogue. Some good examples include Open Space Technology, Appreciative Inquiry, World Café, Visual Explorer, and so on. To that end, here are some must-have published references for the facilitator's toolbox:

- *The Change Handbook* by Holman, Devane, and Cady (2007). The authors, all leading practitioners in the field, offer sixty-one change methods.
- *The Practical Decision Maker* by Harvey et al. (2001). This resource includes fifty-four different structuring devices for problem solving.
- *The Handbook of Large Group Methods* by Bunker and Alban (2006). Just as in their earlier work, *Large Group Interventions*, Bunker and Alban provide a comprehensive overview of the latest methods.

Equally important—while working with or facilitating group efforts—is not only to acquire familiarity with effective meeting designs, but also to balance group tasks against interpersonal relationships. Activities and attention must be appropriately divided between both. We will have more to say on this in chapter 8, "Strategies for Struggle," in connection with Jones and Bearley's notion of a Team Development Matrix.

Action 2: Having thus become acquainted with the available resources, it is now time to craft an engaging plan for an upcoming meeting. The first step is to settle on any desired outcomes, then find a specific design (or fusion of multiple designs) that can move the group from point A to point B. Keep in mind that when designing an agenda, cultivating Standpoint also implies increasing the members' participation. This way individual perspectives can be placed on the table, as it were.

Action 3: Implement and follow through! With everyone's Standpoint in the open and specific actions agreed upon, the members must take appropriate action. Nothing is worse than failing to follow through with commitment; that would indicate only valuable time lost. With failure as the norm, people will feel reluctant to share their Standpoint in any subsequent meetings. At any rate, people get tired of dull meetings in the best of times, especially those that lack structure and show little participation. In this respect, the informational meeting is relatively easy for all concerned, because it requires little planning. Perhaps this is why so many people choose this path.

The news brief approach to staff meetings is a sure path to disappointment, because it runs contrary to the spirit of the PLC by doing exactly the opposite of nurturing Standpoint.

Bringing everyone together for a face-to-face meeting may seem unfeasible for various reasons at first. Perhaps a team or school has to decide immediately, or the district-union bargaining agreement precludes another school-wide meeting that month. A Standpoint on the main issues must be sought even then. If a formal meeting is not possible, then take advantage of online survey tools. This is a quick way to gather people's ideas.

STANDPOINT STRATEGY 4: TAKE TIME TO WALK IN OTHERS' SHOES

Upon returning from summer vacation, a teacher learned that his classroom assignment had been changed and he had been moved to the other side of campus. This news upset him because he had been teaching in the same room for five years. To get an explanation, he marched over to the administration building to speak with the principal.

On entering the front office he noticed a group of teachers also waiting to speak with the principal. After a thirty-five-minute wait, which only compounded his negative attitude, he finally got an opportunity to voice his displeasure. When he faced the principal he noticed the downtrodden cast on her face; she was tired of the unending line of unhappy teachers. Frustrated, he presented his case about the inconvenience of switching rooms. She explained the school's larger goal of establishing a lower house (ninth and tenth grades) and an upper house (eleventh and twelfth grades); therefore, teachers had to be moved closer to others teaching related content to the same batch of students.

This information allowed him to see her point of view. In short, he was able to imagine what she must be going through to help the school be successful. In view of the enormity of her task, not to speak of the likely reluctance of faculty and staff, he decided against picking a fight with her. Instead, he wanted to help her realize the new school vision. She thanked him for being receptive to the change.

This teacher changed his Standpoint because he decided to *take the time to walk in another's shoes*. As German educator Friedrich Ludwig Jahn once said, "The secret of living in peace with all people lies in the art of understanding each one by his own individuality." A corollary of this is that we must recognize the diversity of Standpoint in all people. Working to identify and incorporate member Standpoint into the PLC helps build strong member relationships.

Here are four actions for walking in other people's shoes and strengthening the PLC.

Action 1: When around colleagues, seek to open up communication channels. But choose clarity, concision, and transparency over small talk or gossip. Discourse can tear down the barriers that separate people, allowing us to learn more about each other's motivations and other factors that influence action. We learn about things from others' point of view—namely, their Standpoint.

Action 2: Shared leadership empowers all members of the PLC to achieve a better understanding of the various roles and responsibilities that come with position. Official job descriptions alone rarely tell everything. Sharing leadership, on the other hand, opens the opportunity for a better view of how and why certain decisions are made, giving the members a chance to walk in their colleagues' shoes.

Action 3: Work to promote empathy among all members of the PLC. While most schools have become data driven, they are nevertheless populated by subjective and intuitive members. Remember, walking in someone else's shoes is not limited simply to taking perspective of things; more importantly it implies that the emotional and reactive Standpoints of others, no less than one's own, are understood. Our capacity to recognize and share the feelings of others is an extremely valuable skill to have in a PLC.

Action 4: Sometimes we are too focused. We believe that only we know what is good for the organization. Chuck out the "I am right, and you are wrong" mentality, if it's the last thing you do. Lose the defensiveness and work to appreciate the other person's perspective. Do not blind yourself to possibility. Granted, even after *taking the time to walk in others' shoes* you may never fully understand another member's Standpoint. Still, you should make a special effort to reach out to colleagues to validate the importance of their Standpoint. When people recognize this gesture they will respond in kind and throw in their hat as the team tries to build the strong relationships it needs to be a successful PLC.

STANDPOINT STRATEGY 5: CELEBRATE DIVERSITY OFTEN

Paradoxically, diversity can be a powerful *unifying* force. The etymological root word suggests "splitting." In our present context *diversity* embraces all aspects of the school, including culture and subcultures, perspectives and viewpoints, ways of thinking, and personal idiosyncrasies—hence its unifying possibilities. A school or PLC that displays no diversity whatsoever has no opportunity to learn or improve anything. Researchers have described the diversity behind organizational success as a kind of "creative tension."

Irish president Michael D. Higgins once remarked, "I think the important thing now is to have a celebration and then with determination move into our common, shared, different future." This is tantamount to a concept of creative tension, because it presupposes the need for dissenting views—in essence, diversity—to create an admittedly uncomfortable state but one conducive to solutions.

As a matter of principle, systems always move toward equilibrium, even though equilibrium itself is nothing but a state of nonmovement, whereas, by definition, progress implies movement toward a specific destination. But without creative tension what need is there to move forward, backward, or sideways for a solution? In other words, there must be a certain degree of "disruption" of fixed patterns of thinking and self-interested posturing if the path to a better future is to be plotted. The trick is to find a constructive way to handle these disruptions, to harness them as a unifying force on teams. When all is said and done, diversity ought to be *celebrated*, not banished from our midst.

Action 1: Staff members can celebrate diversity by sharing food dishes and local or ethnic customs. Relationships among staff are not just relationships; they are PLC building blocks. They present invaluable opportunities for the development of a powerful strategy. Celebrating diversity may consist, say, in picking a day to fete the culture and foods of each staff member. Why not organize a good old-fashioned potluck to celebrate Mexican food? Every staff member can bring homemade Mexican dishes. Non-Mexican staff would thoroughly enjoy celebrating Mexican culture; their enjoyment will be greater if they can cook up Mexican dishes of their own. In general, remember to celebrate culturally significant days. Never mind a school-wide celebration every time, as no one will be disappointed if a simple celebratory e-mail makes the rounds.

Action 2: Encourage dissent in meetings. Dissent is particularly useful to a leader trying to present a new idea to staff, on whom he or she should count to figure out the pros and cons of your idea (usually the cons first). It is a strong asset to have. For starters, the list of cons provide leaders with a ready basis for troubleshooting in all new programs or initiatives. Your staff are in a unique position to identify what is wrong before it becomes a problem. Their views may reflect the variety of viewpoints and thinking in both the community and the school. That aside, intellectual diversity can be quite fragile and may require a strong element of trust owing to the fact that success rests on a common yet variegated future for all.

STANDPOINT STRATEGY 6: REFLECT ON YOUR OWN PERSPECTIVES AND HOW OTHERS MAY REACT

While preparing to hold his first faculty meeting at a new school, a new principal planned an icebreaking activity where faculty and staff would be required to break up into small discussion groups. After inspecting the spacious multipurpose room available, he opted for an unused classroom with tables and chairs. The faculty and staff, accustomed to holding meetings in the multipurpose room, quietly murmured their angst about the new principal "already trying to change everything." They wondered what else he was planning.

Somehow the first icebreaking activity proved conducive to a new culture, as he hoped. After that, every subsequent faculty and staff meeting was held in a classroom. Midway through the school year, a teacher took him aside to explain that, despite the initial misgivings of her colleagues regarding the change of venue, their team within the overarching school PLC had grown comfortable. When she told him how everyone now preferred the classroom setting, they laughed about the whole episode. Then the principal had an epiphany about his attitude in the past. Before the first meeting he had been so worked up about presenting his Standpoint that he had failed to anticipate the reaction of faculty and staff.

Reflecting on your perspectives and how others may react encourages members to consider the Standpoint of colleagues and helps establish or solidify relationships. It's okay if you miss the first time. After all, "All ideas come about through some sort of observation. It sparks an attitude; some object or emotion causes a reaction in the other person," as English author and performer Graham Chapman wrote.

The members of a PLC influence each other thanks to their regular interaction. Granted, Standpoint serves as a guide, but one must be cognizant of the reactions it may provoke among colleagues who hold a different Standpoint. One should always seek to anticipate as many reactions as possible.

Below are four actions that leaders may take to reinforce the PLC as they reflect on their perspectives.

Action 1: When working closely with others it is important to be *fully* present. We often get lost in our own thoughts and miss what the other person is saying, or we fail to *act* on how others are thinking or feeling. We need to be more self-aware, of our own thoughts, and more aware of the thoughts, feelings, and reactions of others. So pay attention to how your actions affect others.

Action 2: As you make your decision based on your Standpoint, remember that people will react and decide based on their respective Standpoints. Therefore, try to understand and accept that colleagues will arrive at decisions for reasons that may not necessarily apply to you. Remove the "If I were him, then I would do this" mentality from your head. Instead, think of the member's Standpoint and how he or she will react to your actions. Remember, there are always reasons why something happens; they just may not be ours, and that is okay.

Action 3: Debriefing with colleagues enhances clear thinking. Past or upcoming events and feelings should receive their due. Communication opens people's minds to differing Standpoints they might not have previously considered. It helps them anticipate and prepare for future contingencies.

Action 4: Habituate yourself with examining your Standpoint. Question what you know and how you got to know it. This is a great way both to develop your critical faculty and to compare your Standpoint with that of others. Becoming adept at questioning yourself and others will help you anticipate difficulties before they arise, plan for the future with other members' Standpoints in mind, and more generally improve the current situation of your school.

Thinking too often revolves around what has already happened. Reflecting *forward*, on future action, will enable you to *reflect more clearheadedly on your present perspective and how others may react to it*. As a proactive approach, this should lead to the incorporation of member Standpoints and a stronger ability to predict potential problems or conflicts before they crowd out the solutions.

STANDPOINT STRATEGY 7: STRENGTHEN UNION AND ADMINISTRATION RELATIONSHIPS

Do unions and administrators in your school or district work collaboratively, or have relations become a never-ending "battle royal"? Labor and management relationships have certainly been struggling in every state, district, and school over the decades. Given this long experience, there is no other way to state the risk your institution faces: an "Us vs. Them" mentality will defeat the higher purpose of your PLC.

As American psychologist and philosopher William James wrote, "Whenever you're in conflict with someone, there is one factor that can make the difference between damaging your relationship and deepening it. That factor is attitude." It goes without saying.

Think of it this way: how could a school that is bustling with togetherness and genuine collaboration but suffering from recurrent labor-related tensions achieve the level of a PLC? The two antagonists—union and administration—must first find a way to bury their hatchets, soothe frayed egos, and work on issues of concern to all. Ideally, PLC management and unions trust one another and appreciate one another's Standpoint. But this is an achievable ideal. After all, why should students have to end up with the short end of the stick every time the administration and union deem it fitting to bicker back and forth?

Where do you situate yourself in this? Are you part of the problem or the solution?

Action 1: District superintendents (joined by their cabinet members) and union leadership have to make a special effort to model expected behavior. The two rival factions have to come together regularly to deal with district-wide concerns, issues, or more serious problems. In the end, this relationship has to be win-win for all parties concerned, with the exclusion of no one.

Some districts can truly be said to have adopted this course of action. Nearly ten years ago, for instance, the San Bernardino City Unified School District in California cobbled together a solution-generating team they named "Creating Opportunities—One Purpose" (CO-OP). This team comprised the key stakeholders: superintendent and assistant superintendents, union president and vice president, a principal representative for each level (elementary, middle, and high), and a handful of teachers. Half- to full-day meetings occurred monthly on some of the toughest issues. While everyone's Standpoint was considered, titles lost their relevancy. In tough times, with budget cuts as deep as the sea, the team was able to address a $44 million budget deficit in only one year.

Another interesting district in California was ABC Unified School District. In his research article, "Toward Collaboration in District/Association Relationships: ABC School District," Harvey (2009) explained, "District superintendent and president of the association meet every week for two hours. District cabinet and association cabinet meet two-three times a year and talk confidentially. The association has converted building representatives into learning representatives" (p. 1). He described their four conflict-resolution principles thus:

1. They both have an interest to cooperate and a capacity to compete.
2. They have norms.
3. They have mutual trust born out of interdependence.
4. They look for the middle ground of agreement.

Action 2: Principals and teachers at the site level should fortify their relationships by working in unison to find solutions to site-specific problems. But there is no way around it: both parties have to hold one another accountable for commitments and actively work for students' best interests, above all.

Action 3: Principals and teachers should study and fully understand their district bargaining agreement. Unfortunately, too few have any clue of what their agreements actually read. A lack of understanding leads to frayed relationships and multiplying grievances.

The main strategy here—*strengthening union and administration relationships*—requires not necessarily the deep commitment of limited financial resources, but more importantly a sincere investment of time and positive attitude from all involved parties to work toward the betterment of the overall organization.

STANDPOINT STRATEGY 8: LEARN THE HISTORICAL AND POLITICAL HISTORY OF THE SCHOOL AND COMMUNITY

Every school has a unique history. Communicating that history in an orderly, accurate fashion can be a challenge. Staff no doubt will seek to brief the new administrator on the "way things are." The intention may be honorable, but this manner inevitably pushes political perspectives to the forefront. As one former superintendent said upon retiring after eleven years in the same district, "Superintendents and principals do not get fired for API, test scores, or A-G rates. They get fired because they don't understand the power and politics in the district." This is because their fate is a function of their level of understanding of the historical and political history of the school. The importance of politics and history cannot be overestimated.

This is true with every succession from a beloved but retiring principal to an unknown quantity. In our example, the previous principal had stabilized relationships within the current power structure and, generally, conducted himself in a certain way, to which staff had become accustomed. It would be facile for a new leader to attempt to fill his chair while disregarding the fundamental power structure reigning in the school. How many an administrator has been dismissed for lack of political sense.

African American civil rights leader Martin Luther King, Jr., clearly saw this. "We are not makers of history. We are made by history," he proclaimed. We need to appreciate these words. History exerts its own power over people, in part because it can shed light on who they are and why they do certain things as individual employees and as a school. New PLC members have to question their motives and Standpoints, and tenured PLC members need to reflect on the factors of their success.

But who are the historians? Who is best placed to explain the politics and history of the school? For that to happen the narrative must somehow connect various perspectives. A challenge in the best of times, but one has to start somewhere. The best starting point is listening and posing questions back and forth. This can only be a drawn-out process, because no one has a perfect rearview image; therefore, no single person ought to monopolize history telling.

Action 1: Take the time to listen to what the office staff or the secretary says. The head office is the school's nerve center. Its employees can serve as an invaluable resource on the school's political and historical background. In fact, the next time you go to the office, pick up some sweets on the way. It's a marvelous way to "butter up" the employees on whom you depend for information. After talking to the secretary and office staff, a picture of the school will emerge, but that hardly means you should stop investigating the full history of the school or asking questions altogether. Veterans should be your next priority. Thanks to their tenure, veteran teachers have an insider's view, which may differ from that of other teachers. Talk to a few from every side about the history and politics of the school.

Action 2: Start the day by greeting veteran staff with a pleasant hello, before going to the veteran teachers' classrooms for a chat. If you need advice on a specific matter, seek out a veteran. Ask him about the present situation, as well as what he recalls of the past. Learning the politics and history of your school and community will improve your prospects of success. Strategy 8 is anchored in this type of knowledge. Short of that, any effort to improve circumstances will be in vain. The truth is cultural and political landscapes change constantly. What worked before may not anymore. So if you seek to revive your PLC, take the politics and history of your school seriously. They are indispensable to bringing solid and hopefully irreversible success to your institution.

II

Struggle

> Individuals vested in improving student achievement through ongoing dialogue wrapped with data to support next steps in the teaching process. Forums must be created within the school day for educators to engage in conversations about teaching and learning to ensure best practices are in place for the kids we serve. This means committing time, committing energy, and committing to engaging with one another to advance learning of all kids in our charge.
> —Kelly J. Meyers, associate executive director, Association of Wisconsin School Administrators

Standpoint is to the heart of PLC what Struggle (figure p. II, which applies to the second quadrant in the 4S Approach) is to a heart arrhythmia. Without proper preventive and prescriptive measures it can be unsettling, and it can damage the quadrants in our model. Unregulated Struggle will arrest all progress and benefit accruing from the recognition and incorporation of Standpoint. In the context of the 4S Approach, Standpoint itself gives rise to conflict, sometimes over scarce resources but mostly due to the diversity of opinions, personalities, experiences, and skills among the members. Given that no two members' Standpoint are alike, opposing outlooks are almost inevitable.

For argument's sake, though, try to imagine a world without Struggle. It would be nice for everyone to get along and think the same. What pressing need would there be to collaborate if the Standpoint of the one stands for the Standpoint of all? Uniformity would be the norm. We all long for peace and harmony in the world. The paradox is that without friction and opposing viewpoints, complacency and stagnation tend to set in, thus limiting the school's capacity for innovation and compromising its success. Schools develop as PLCs through the recognition, discussion, and defense of Standpoint.

The next three chapters discuss the possible outcomes of Struggle. Chapter 6 ("May Day! Mayday!") focuses on their damaging impact; the chapter that follows ("Stakes and Standpoint") examines the outcomes

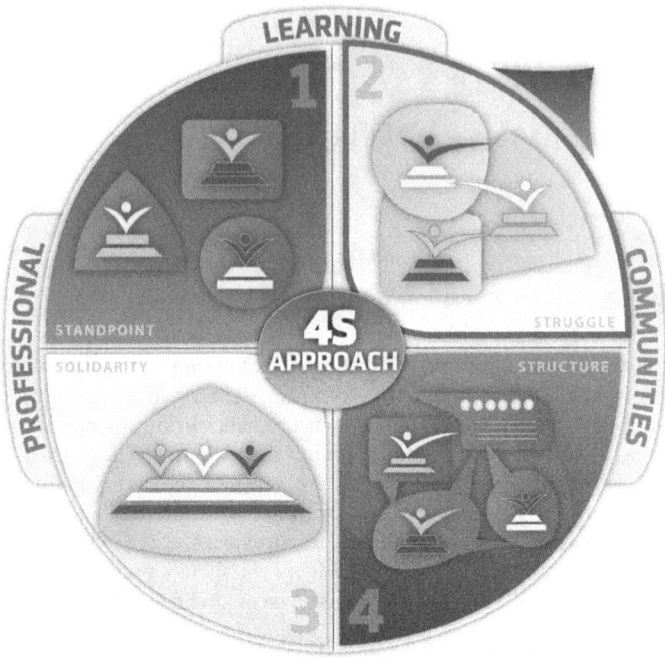

Figure 5.2. The 4S Approach—Struggle

associated with diverse perspectives and goals. Finally, chapter 8 ("Strategies for Struggle") details eight actions to confront and overcome Struggle in your school.

SIX
May Day! Mayday!

> The realization has hit home that we are all responsible for every student's academic success!
>
> —Diand Canipe, principal, Lincolnton, NC

A few years ago the administrators of a school called an emergency faculty meeting at the end of the school day to discuss students mimicking the May Day protests that were taking place at city halls nationwide. Youths were inspired by daily televised reports and had begun to walk out of classrooms and the campus. Far from understanding the reasoning behind the protests, many students saw them as an opportunity to have some fun or cause trouble.

The administration called a sixty-minute meeting to come up with ways to keep the students inside and off the streets. Unfortunately, the meeting failed to bring agreement among faculty on how to approach the students' actions. The social studies teachers felt the students had a right to protest, given the peaceful nature of their demonstrations. The math teachers were, for their part, fixated on the average daily attendance they claimed the school was losing with the student walkout. The English teachers wanted the students to use the events as material for their reflective journals, while the physical education instructors argued that if the students ran more laps they would be too tired to walk off campus.

Although the general opinion among faculty concurred in the disruptiveness of the student protests, there seemed little agreement on how to handle the situation. Some even advanced a strong-handed approach that included local law enforcement issuing tickets and fines to the protestors. If any student missed any class work, they suggested, that student should not be allowed to make it up. To seal the deal they suggested a daily quiz, which the protesting students would not be permitted to make up. The administration further wanted all the doors closed during class time to keep the students from sneaking out while the teachers' backs were turned. One administrator even floated the idea of having teachers stand near the doors.

At this point of the meeting, a petite science teacher spoke up. She had serious reservations about "standing near the door," as her smaller size would hardly discourage the male students; worse, she told the members, acting as a physical barrier might place her in harm's way. "There is no way I am going to be able to stop some big black boys from walking out the door."

Hearing this, several African American teachers objected to a white teacher singling out the "big black boys." One upset female African American teacher declared that she could very well be a parent of one of those "big black boys," being a mother herself. The other African Americans also took her to task, which only upset the petite teacher. Her cheeks reddened and her eyes welled with tears. Unable to express herself and embarrassed, she raced out of the meeting. Seeing this, her colleagues from the science department felt bound to defend her, insisting she was not racist. They pointed out that the majority of the students on this campus were African American, that her remark was based on a simple statistical fact, and therefore that this was nothing more than a miscommunication blown out of proportion.

As the voices grew louder and the discussion more heated, two factions began to distinguish themselves. On the one side, science teachers tried to clarify a colleague's misspoken words; on the other, African American teachers verbalized their discontent and hurt. And back and forth it all went for the rest of the meeting, with everyone talking over the other and a handful standing aloof in disbelief wondering what had just happened. The meeting quickly lost its focus on the original objective: figuring out how to keep the students in the classrooms and off the streets.

True, diversity was plainly obvious just from their physical appearances. But what they needed was an honest effort to acknowledge others' Standpoints, not just their racial origins. Physical appearance does not exhaust diversity. Besides skin color, personal and work experiences, opinion, ethnicity, language, and custom give manifestation to diversity. And yet a superficial allusion to race can trounce all these characteristics. The science teacher's remark seemed to accomplish exactly that by provoking a deep-seated fear of discrimination based on skin color.

As things stood, the range of Standpoints among the group members, if not properly addressed, threatened to take the group away from the effective, productive unit its members had aspired to and to generalize its state of dysfunction. Instead of moving forward, the team risked getting bogged down in a new Struggle over claims of racism and miscommunication. The result? After sixty minutes the faculty found itself no closer to finding a solution than when the meeting had convened. Only now, a new problem had come into view that seemed to throw future collaboration in doubt. Reflexively, the administrators made a point of not mentioning the incident in subsequent meetings and everyone acted as if nothing had ever happened.

The key word here is "acted," because the tension remained noticeably high as the faculty relived the incident, again and again, and quietly eyed the science teacher and the African American faculty who had taken her to task. Fearing another similar incident, fewer and fewer teachers spoke at the meetings. Gone was the spirit of inclusion, along with the very heart of the PLC. What remained was a group paralyzed and afraid to interact because of a vaguely defined conflict.

As PLCs continue to develop, schools have found new opportunities to move toward team-based assignments for their members. To cope with the requirements of the twenty-first-century marketplace, many organizations have shifted completely to team-based work (King, Hebl, & Beal, 2009)—after all, *we are smarter than me*. But this has placed the onus all the more on them to understand the nature of the Struggle; no one else will find a coherent way to work through Struggle. That said, this quadrant is about more than just group and team dynamics.

With proper awareness and understanding the synergy level will grow, allowing the members to make the most of an uncomfortable situation. Not all viewpoints will harmonize, to be sure, but then trying to fit a square peg into a round hole is pointless under any circumstance.

The three most common causes of Struggle are poor communication systems, inconsiderate behaviors, and ineffective processes. All of them were present in the incident with the science teacher. To recapitulate, she expressed her concern before the faculty rather poorly; this caused resentment among a group of African American teachers; the meeting was ineffectively facilitated by the administrators.

Although few other faculty members were involved in this dispute, it affected the entire learning community. Clashes and dysfunctions are inevitable in groups charged with multiple tasks. But while Struggle is a natural part of group life, the future of every PLC hinges on its staff's ability to overcome dysfunctions and to work together productively with a view to improving learning for all.

Imagine a group member acting out her dissatisfaction on others. Now ask yourself: How is this individual affecting the team? Is there a particular reason for her behavior? Perhaps she is passing through a divorce, or has recently been diagnosed with depression. Maybe the cause of the depression is work-related stress, in which case: How is that person's health holding back the team? Suppose the principal had unexpectedly announced an extra ten thousand dollars for the school. A welcome surprise, no doubt, but how will it be distributed? Who will select the recipients? How was the sum determined? How will the groups now competing for the money view and interact with one another? How will the decision, when it comes, affect the overall morale and strength of the PLC?

STRUGGLE IS NORMAL

Few people sanely choose either Struggle or the heightened emotions, tense looks, and discomfort it brings in its wake. In a perfect world, perhaps, everyone would be living and working in peace and harmony. But where in the real world are there two people living or working together over a long period of time who agree on, literally, everything? An absence of conflict more likely suggests that one of them has suppressed or continually subordinates her views to the other. This acquiescence might at first seem acceptable over the short term, but in the long haul it will raise the level of anger and resentment to a point where the Struggle, when it finally surfaces, will be very intense.

In the literature teams and the role diversity plays in their development have been widely studied. As noted by Weeks (1994), "Conflict is an inescapable part of daily lives, and inevitable result of our highly complex, competitive, and often litigious society" (p. ix). Levi (2007) considered conflict a normal and integral part of a team-development process. Despite the normality, teams are usually unwilling or uncomfortable in dealing with Struggle. Given the unavoidable nature of conflict, however, getting a grip on the structure and ingredients of conflict resolution is critical to successful team development.

Many studies on work teams have shown that the impact of conflict depends both on its type and the diversity of the team (Jehn, 1995). The strategies described in chapter 5 can help minimize conflicts in the future by incorporating member Standpoints, as long as the organization's goals, as a whole, function to draw focus away from individual Standpoints toward a more global position with which all or most members could identify.

Organizational diversity encompasses differences in organizational position, occupation, and subculture (Levi, 2007, p. 231; Northcraft et al., 1995). In other words, the more hierarchical an organizational structure is the greater the opportunities for internal diversity, and the better the likelihood for Struggle. As we know, schools are hierarchical with primarily top-down, administrative or district mandates that permit the teachers to develop a certain camaraderie against the top-down leadership. This is congenial to a culture of Them vs. Us, because teachers may feel constrained or persecuted by the new mandates. A Them vs. Us mentality will only exacerbate the Struggle.

Another common design flaw in educational structure is due to teachers who spend their entire day inside the classroom, interacting only with students. Many teachers eat lunch inside their classrooms or use break time to plan lessons, correct assignments, or communicate with parents, all of which furthers their isolation. They do this because they feel they are doing just fine on their own. Having taught the same grade or curriculum for years, they are likely to resist any change offered collaboratively by the PLC. As a result, change initiatives that touch on grade level, curriculum, or teaching strategy are generally met with Struggle. The higher the stakes the more entrenched the members become, and the greater the likelihood of Struggle.

Compounding the difficulties associated with the hierarchical mentality is the individual member Standpoint. It can amount to a breeding ground for a host of unresolved issues. Members will be quite eager to get their fair share when every school dollar matters. The truth is that their competing interests will clash under conditions where money and other resources are limited—or worse, scarce. Only if school professionals can work through their Struggle in groups will their collective intelligence emerge. Group wisdom surpasses that of any individual effort.

Clearly, a PLC depends on how individuals and groups respond to everything discordant in their midst, though without arrogating to themselves the power to eliminate all conflict.

SEVEN
Stakes and Standpoint

> A PLC allows teachers the ability to work as a group to commonly plan and work as a team while lessening the burden on individual teachers.
> —Dr. James Norwood, teacher, Moreno Valley, CA

As staff and faculty try to move toward a true PLC culture, diverse member viewpoints act as precursors to conflict, or Struggle. But the transition from isolation to collaboration can be arduous. A school cannot simply declare itself a PLC school and then all is well and good.

If you are seeking to turn your school's culture into one of collaboration and cooperation, be forewarned about the many growing pains. But it is certainly worth the effort—in fact, the growing never quite stops. For one thing, members routinely enter and leave the payroll. Every change in personnel brings a new Standpoint and the potential for Struggle. Just as each school and organization has its unique persona and culture, shaped primarily by its members' Standpoints, so too will it manifest its unique Struggle.

STAKES AND STANDPOINT BREED STRUGGLE

As the group gets bigger, the risks increase exponentially. When I am alone planning to go to lunch, my choice of place and type of food is limited by three things: my imagination, the time available, and the money I want to spend. If I want join a colleague for lunch, I keep in mind that we share the same three limitations, albeit from differing Standpoints. This is important even though the added perspective complicates my decision. It may happen that we instantly agree on the location; most of the time we discuss it a little before finding a compromise. None of this is a big deal if we are friends and the stakes are relatively low with no lasting impact. We are just going to lunch, right?

Say a third person joins us. Same three limitations; only now, the conversation becomes a notch more complex. But while the decision calls for a three-way negotiation, not just compromise, Struggle is still negligible, because we happen also to be good friends and the stakes are low. It is just lunch. As the group grows in size Standpoint becomes more diverse. The same limitations persist, but the possibilities pose a new challenge.

Efficacy of communication and compromise stand in proportion to the size of the group. Larger groups need to work on clear and concise communication if vital information is to reach all members in the most accurate manner possible. The more Standpoints exist in the group the greater the chance for miscommunication and misunderstanding—and the bigger the chance of conflict.

With higher stakes the willingness to compromise declines, because every solution, every decision contemplated has consequence. This state of affairs renders the members more rigid. Personally, I have no problem settling for Italian food with a colleague for lunch, even if originally I had a stronger hankering for Mexican food. I just say to myself, we can always get burritos the next time. Why? Because going for lunch is a low-stakes issue. But that does not mean that I have no desire to be heard, understood, and respected by the staff and faculty purporting to be developing a new school-wide mission statement, or some other high-stakes issue.

The bottom line is that I am little inclined to settle for anyone else's solution or decision. I want to be heard *now*, not "next time" when the issue is so much "water under the bridge." Struggle is rarely about a future problem; most of the time it has to do with differing perceptions of an actual situation and with the fear that someone wants to run roughshod over individual Standpoints.

The benefits of having, recognizing, and incorporating diverse Standpoints in a team or organization are truly impressive. Levi (2007) insisted that the multiple skills and perspectives brought together within decision-making processes make all the difference. Granted, every time the PLC members get together for a major decision, their differing Standpoints have the potential of creating the conditions for Struggle. But perception can be tricky. Some members seek to learn the "Big Picture" before choosing a course of action. Others concern themselves with bringing everyone into the fold and, basically, swimming with the flow. Still others push their own agenda with little regard for the Big Picture, or for that matter, the concerns of fellow team members.

A further faction may accept the Big Picture while secretly advancing their own agendas. However, it is not diversity that causes the Struggle, but the thoughts and actions of the individual members. Typically, members pursue interests that compete with those of their colleagues. Everyone has his or her own motivation for thinking and acting in a certain manner. Improperly handled, this can easily muddle or clog the process. Schools need to learn to embrace Struggle in their organization as they work to overcome the challenges, not the reverse.

According to Sawyer, Houlette, and Yeagley (2006), the structure of group diversity determines the *effect* of diversity rather than its extent. How many types of members here is less important than the effect they allow their differences to have inside the group. Should an individual Standpoint take center stage, in place of the common purposes, goals, and overall success of the organization, Struggle will take on an unseemly form.

In this sense, one bad apple will spoil the bunch.

CAUSE OF STRUGGLE

Struggle generally revolves around a disagreement between two or more parties. In the previous example, I mentioned three limitations on my decision: imagination, available time, and cost expectation. These limitations are true of organizations too. Member Standpoints spur the imagination and thus give rise to possibilities; increasing the number of team members increases the competition over the organization's limited resources of time and money, since not every member will get what he asks for.

Miscommunication and misunderstanding among PLC members can only compound the Struggle. To minimize them the members have to try hard to communicate with one another as concisely and accurately as possible. This offers the best chance to identify the real cause of an ongoing Struggle. As Levi (2007) argued, "Determining the root cause of the conflict will aid the team's development and not waste time" (p. 113). As a normal part of PLC and organizational life Struggle allows the parties to identify and compete for limited options and finite resources. Those parties need now to inventory the "possibilities" that the members have devised and developed in their role as a cohesive problem-solving team.

There is no way around it: one must simply look past the current conflict to find the root cause of the Struggle, the object being to meet the Struggle head on, not discount or ignore it.

NEGATIVE OUTCOMES FROM STRUGGLE

There is a persistent tendency to view Struggle solely as a negative experience. PLC members rightfully distrust difficult individuals or circumstances, but complete avoidance of conflict is not possible.

Here are some of the negative outcomes of Struggle:

1. *Wasted resources (time, money, personnel, and energy) spent on handling and generally dealing with a conflict.* Instead of spending time in meetings developing and strengthening the PLC, members focus on a temporary dispute to determine who is "right" and who is "wrong" and to place blame.
2. *Wasted resources and poor decision making, resulting in decreased productivity and little time or focus for planning and guiding the school toward its goals.* What decisions are taken in response usually revolve around putting an end to the Struggle.
3. *Permanent erosion of personal, work, and community relationships.* This results in lower motivation and morale, which in turn lead to a level of Struggle that leaves PLC members dissatisfied and stressed out. Left untreated, Struggle produces lasting emotional and psychological scars that can stunt the development of the PLC. Under these conditions distrust and mutual hostility will heavily influence future interactions.
4. *Toxic air inside an organization.* This is indicative of the level of withdrawal, miscommunication, or downright noncommunication among the members. Instead of working to resolve the Struggle, many members prefer to sit out every storm. Others do the opposite and focus on the Struggle instead of on trying to find a proper solution to the dispute. Members spend their time complaining, blaming, backstabbing, and gossiping about their colleagues.
5. *What happens to one happens to all, because the PLC functions on principles of collaboration and communication.* Struggle may at first threaten the interests of the parties to the dispute, but in time the harm will reach even those not directly involved. Like a spreading cancer, Struggle may eventually consume every member of the PLC—staff, faculty, and involved community members.

BENEFITS OF STRUGGLE

Successfully overcoming a Struggle through better understanding and insight presents new opportunities for both individual and collective growth. The experience of Struggle allows the group to strengthen the team in the following ways:

1. *Creation of new ideas.* Struggle forces members to see things in a new light. It is not easy to recognize new ideas in the thick of a heated confrontation, to be sure. It requires patient attention and, in some instances, entirely new ways of seeing things through the arguments and points scored in the course of the dispute. Focusing and actively listening to others are crucial to a felicitous outcome of Struggle.

2. *Learning about team members.* Struggle is a great way for members to learn more about their colleagues' experiences and beliefs. With proper attention the members can pick up loads of information about one another.
3. *Increased awareness of personal Standpoint.* A surprising benefit of Struggle is the opportunity it affords team members to learn about themselves. After all, they should have a chance for personal reflection well before having to defend their Standpoints. Members learn about their own beliefs regarding a particular topic and why they hold them. Discussions allow them to raise points and defend issues until they can fathom their personal biases and capacity to take criticism.
4. *Ability to accept different perspectives.* Engaging in Struggle gives members the chance to confront perspectives different from their own in a constructive way, so long as they remain open-minded. It may be perfectly legitimate to differ in one's Standpoint, but little good will come of it if one cannot keep an open mind or be willing to hear what others have to say. Members do not have to agree completely—or at all, for that matter—with those perspectives, but at least an effort to acknowledge the differences and validate them will have been made.
5. *Practice in communicating.* Effective communication is critical to positive action and dealing with Struggle. The more members engage in healthy discussion, the more opportunity they have for practice and the development of effective communication skills.

EIGHT
Strategies for Struggle

> The development of effective PLC initiatives in districts depends upon clarity of its purpose, the support and cooperation of all staff members, adequate time to meet, and agreed upon protocols for facilitating the collaborative work of the group.
> —Dr. Sheryl S. Solow, assistant superintendent, Montrose, CO

WHAT EMPOWERING STRATEGIES MAKE PLCS SUCCESSFUL?

This chapter contains eight practical strategies for PLC members to overcome the often paralyzing consequences of Struggle (figure 8.1). Ignoring them usually leads to dissension and stagnation.

1. Be honest and transparent, even through difficult conversations.
2. Balance task and relationship.
3. Build school-wide agreements and address previous conflict.
4. Concentrate on the mission and vision, the Big Picture.
5. Focus on the problem, not the individual.
6. Work through differences to solve problems.
7. Seek agreement and communicate the reasoning behind decisions.
8. Apologize meaningfully.

STRUGGLE STRATEGY 1: BE HONEST AND TRANSPARENT, EVEN THROUGH DIFFICULT CONVERSATIONS

Honesty and transparency are foundational values that every leader should exhibit. *Leadership* implies influence, and *influence* flows from strong relationships. *Relationships* are built on trust, while *trust* comes from honesty and transparency.

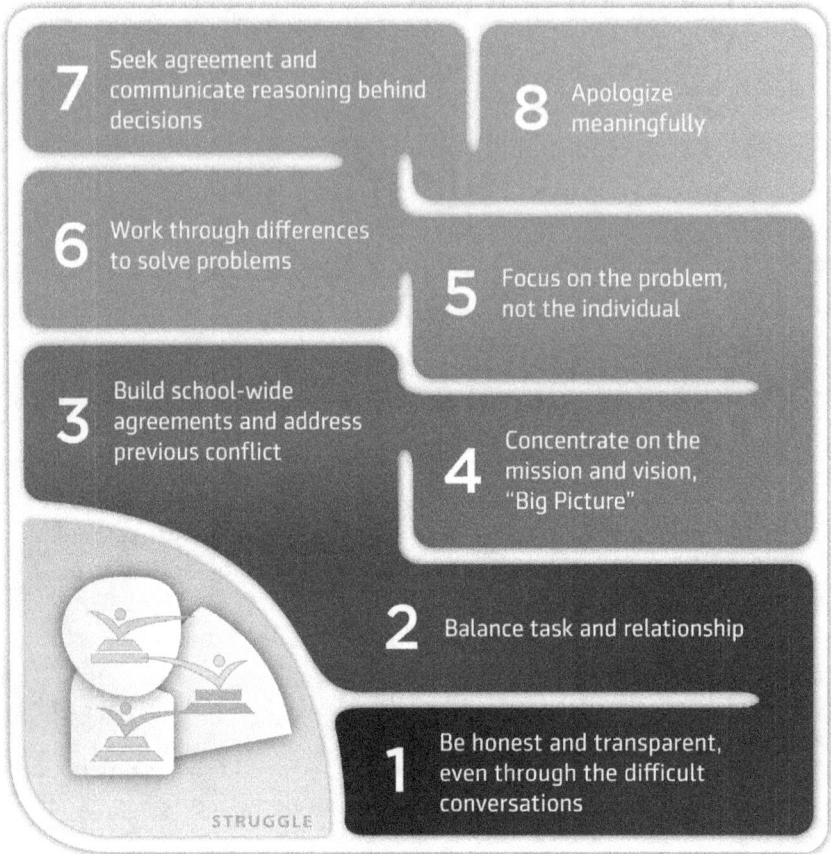

Figure 8.1. Eight Strategies for Struggle

It is a simple cause-and-effect chain, one that conversely may allow dishonesty to chip away at personal integrity. Whereas a faltering industry may turn around eventually, trust—once lost—is extremely hard to rebuild. Some problems—honesty at the helm—just can't be fixed after the fact.

At first blush honesty seems easy enough to define. But would you place "tact" in the same category? For example, a wife asks her husband if a brand-new outfit makes her look terrible. His first response might be, "Good God! You look like a giant grape." It's his most honest opinion, just not very tactful. An honest *and* tactful response might be, "That color isn't my favorite. Why don't you try a different color?"

One message is constructive, the other destructive.

Honesty in a school environment must be delivered with tact. Preserving the dignity of the members preserves relationships. In recognition of this, American industrial designer Freeman Thomas said, "Good design begins with honesty, asks tough questions, comes from collaboration and from trusting your intuition."

He had the right idea, not just on automobile design but on every area of collective activity. Honesty is central to education. In order to reach the goals they profess to uphold, the PLC members must be honest with themselves and with one another.

Action 1: Think before you speak. It never hurts to say, "Let me think about that and get back to you." Take a few moments to think about how best to answer. Another way to encourage a response that is as honest and constructive as yours is simply to frame your initial answer as a personal viewpoint. Say, "This is only my opinion and I don't want to hurt any feelings. Is it okay if I give you this feedback?" Find a way to be honest yet not hurtful. Think about the impact of your words.

Small decisions are easy to frame honestly and positively. Bigger decisions are a different matter, because sometimes there is never a good way to frame bad news. The "bad news" may be a tough conversation that took place at the end of a bad day; the conversation may have been about performance, attitude, or aptitude. When it occurs be compassionate.

Action 2: Be kind but honest. Honesty is one of the most important virtues, even in an uncomfortable conversation—or perhaps, *especially* in an uncomfortable conversation. Would you rather have no one tell you of a shortcoming in your performance, or otherwise be honest with you when something is not right? Still, it is important how we talk to people. Being kind will put you in a position where you can expect the same from others.

One large impediment to honesty is motive. When speaking with staff about a particular issue, the question might crop up, "Why are you telling me this? What about so and so; they are doing the same thing? Why don't you tell them something?" A common reflex to this piece of uncomfortable yet honest feedback is to assume a defensive position. Staff members who get defensive tend to question their critics' motives. Show them your motives. Clarify your thinking as much as possible. Use observable facts and data to illustrate your motives.

Action 3: Explain your thinking and use observable facts. During a particularly tough exchange, remain honest and kind at all times; explain to the person why the conversation has reached this point. Talk to him or her about what you have observed, the facts in your possession, and your train of thought. Make both the conversation and what led up to it completely transparent. In the absence of facts people are naturally inclined to fill in the blanks, but hurt feelings or fear can skew their perceptions. Leave no gap in the conversation to be filled in by rumor.

Every decision is an opportunity to demonstrate the core values and character you wish to show your staff the most. As a strategy, *being honest and transparent even through difficult conversations* will afford you the time to reflect on how you want to be viewed as a member of the PLC. Express your core values with your actions, and then go about your work with deliberation. Honesty and transparency should rank among your core values. Easy or not, they are essential to building a powerful PLC and should be expressed in conversations.

From another angle, there must be constant emphasis on student learning. There will surely be distractions from the course of change upon which the school PLC has embarked. But all through the process honesty and transparency are paramount to reviving and building support for change initiatives.

STRUGGLE STRATEGY 2: BALANCE TASK AND RELATIONSHIP

Schools staff and faculty gather regularly to complete various tasks—such as incorporating enrichment programs as a daily practice, or developing and implementing an acknowledgment system that appreciates students' efforts. The list of must-dos and may-dos can be endless.

Some groups can operate at high levels and, as a result, are able to complete whatever task is put to them in a timely manner. Others fail miserably. Where does the problem lie? Has the task caused too much anxiety? Why has the group been unable to overcome the natural Struggle taking place inside the PLC?

In their article, "Facilitating Team Development," Jones and Bearley (2001) connected task and relationship to group effectiveness: "Sometimes teams sacrifice the task for internal calm, and sometimes teams sacrifice human relations in the service of *getting the job done*" (p. 57). Thus, rather than forgo one or the other, groups ought to give equal consideration to the job at hand and interpersonal rapport inside the group.

To illustrate their argument, they created the Team Development Matrix (figure 8.2). They claim this model offers a sure path to groups aiming to become cohesive, effective teams. By balancing task and relationship, on the one hand, and progressing "on track" and up the diagonal, groups gain in synergy, shared decision making, and collaboration. Short of this, dysfunction (ranging from "one-way" to "flying circus" communication) starts to set in.

This model is pretty straightforward. Too much focus on a task can fray relationships, but focus solely on relationships and nothing will get done. Another notable aspect of the Team Development Matrix is that groups naturally move back to "Square One" each time the group has to cope with its newness, along with its "new tasks, new members, a new leader, etc." (p. 59). It's a dynamic model.

Here are three actions to help teams understand the matrix and overcome Struggle.

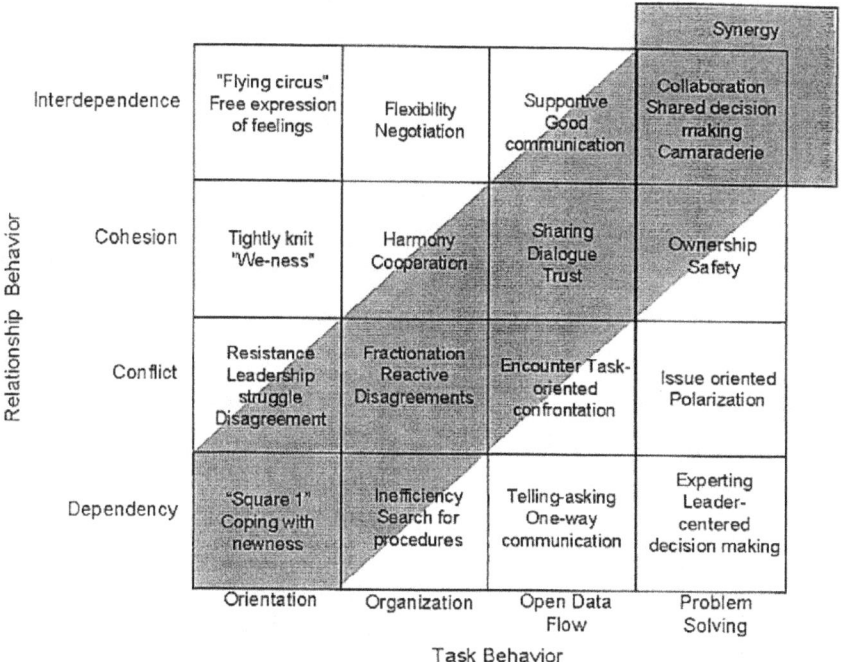

Figure 8.2. Team Development Matrix. Courtesy of Dr. William Bearley. Reprinted with permission.

Action 1: Far too many principals and teachers entertain a shallow understanding of group dynamics and development. The first step in a strategy to *balance task and relationship* is to introduce Jones and Bearley's Team Development Matrix. It is an easy framework to follow, especially if a handful of generic examples can be offered where groups tend to spend too much time on tasking or relationships. Prepare to discuss various scenarios and their rankings on the matrix.

Action 2: Next, gather the members of every group in the school (work groups, teams, and committees) and evaluate their current maturity levels relative to the Team Development Matrix. Here are some straightforward questions each group should answer cooperatively:

1. Where has the team been in the past?
2. Where are they now?
3. Where do they want to be?

The authors also offer an instrument, the Group Development Assessment (GDA), that allows group members to assess how they are functioning in relation to task and relationship dimensions. This tool can be accessed at www.hrdqstore.com.

Action 3: The last step toward maintaining the symmetry between task and relationship is to have each assigned group come together often to evaluate their level of "teamness" and develop strategies to get "back on track" and moving up the diagonal.

Though mostly generic, the questions and the planning outlined in the above actions, it should be noted, can be adapted to the vision, challenges, and direction of any school or group. However, the members of a group must understand what happens when either the task or the relationships are ignored. The strategy of *balancing task and relationship* will help PLC members stay on track, whether it is task or relationship related.

STRUGGLE STRATEGY 3: BUILD SCHOOL-WIDE AGREEMENTS AND ADDRESS PREVIOUS CONFLICT

Practically every school in the country has, at one time or other, suffered unwanted Struggle stemming from unproductive behavior. The conflict may revolve around some unprofessional e-mails or be driven by PLC members who are not conscientious enough to complete their tasks, followed by verbal altercations, uncommunicativeness, nonverbal negative cues, denial of support, rumor mongering, and so on. Such negative behaviors result in ineffective processes, reduced communication, and poor working relationships—the selfsame dynamics we have said impeded PLC progress.

According to retired NFL head coach Tom Flores, "A total commitment is paramount to reaching the ultimate in performance." This assertion acknowledges the need for total commitment and agreement from every party and member if the organization is to be successful. Further, members have to demonstrate their commitment through both words and deeds.

Both productive and unnecessary behaviors are heavily influenced by individual experience, worldview, values, and opinions—in short, by the member's Standpoint. But there are only two choices for eliminating behaviors that hinder progress. The first is the "BB-gun" line of attack, where the administration holds members who fail to meet expectations firmly accountable and imposes disciplinary action. This is done to make sure word got around about unacceptable behavior. Yet, without a clear view of school-wide expectations, such an approach could prove to be a roadblock to Standpoint Strategy 7 (Strengthen union and administration relationships).

The second option is definable more as a "shotgun approach" aimed at *building school-wide agreements.* However, it seeks carefully negotiated standards of behavior. In other words, staff comes together as a group to find a clear agreement (or commitment) on how employees should be expected to behave. Their shared commitments eliminate ambiguity and serve as a guidepost for each member to deal deliberately, conscientiously, and productively with any situation.

Here are some simple, pertinent statements that may be incorporated in any school-wide agreement:

1. Stay open to suggestions.
2. Don't take things personally.
3. Show respect for all.
4. Value the ideas of others.
5. Keep humor and have fun.

The list is endless. Your group may come up with any number of standards adapted to your particular situation. The object is to make explicit the core values of the school. What, then, are the highest leverage behaviors that will lead to success in your PLC?

Action 1: Place everyone in groups of six to eight with chairs arranged in a circle. Assign a tape recorder to someone in each group who has the necessary skill to keep the conversation on track. Part of that person's task is also to list—preferably on a poster-size sheet placed in the middle of the circle—how each group member envisions the points of agreement.

Action 2: Each member receives an index card on which to describe the agreement or protocol most conducive to a school culture of collegiality and group effort. After that the members share their desired agreement aloud. After each statement the person recording asks if everyone in the group has understood and agrees with the norm of the protocol or had reservations. The group continues to share ideas on the desired norms until all the cards have been considered.

Action 3: All the groups come together after their conversations end for a larger meeting, where the recorders briefly summarize their respective groups' exchanges and post their sheets for all to see. Everyone is assigned a partner and each group given ten colored dots. Ask them to walk around the room (in the manner of a gallery walk), exchange ideas on the various norms, and vote on those ideas they jointly feel would best contribute to a positive organizational climate and culture.

Action 4: Count the number of dots for each desired norm. Announce roughly the top ten norms that serve as the initial guideposts for accepted behavior; then ask if anyone has difficulty committing to the newly established norms.

Action 5: Hold one another accountable on the agreements adopted by everyone, but re-form and revisit agreements whenever necessary.

This is only one of hundreds of meeting designs and processes by which staff can build school-wide agreements. The resources available in Standpoint Strategy 3 will be of great assistance.

STRUGGLE STRATEGY 4: CONCENTRATE ON THE MISSION AND VISION, THE BIG PICTURE

The staff and faculty were sad to see their beloved principal promoted to the district level at the end of the school year. The following September the new principal adopted a new target for the school: students have to improve their state standardized test scores. She outlined her plan at the first meeting.

It was determined that the second period would be the students' "homeroom." Once a week, on the students' late-start Wednesdays, the homeroom teacher would concentrate on an activity geared to the state test. The first four Wednesdays would be used to review student scores from the previous year; plus, individual meetings would be held with students in order to build up a sense of accountability. The year progressed, with Wednesdays devoted to reviewing language that is test-question-specific as well as test-taking strategies.

By April a culture of test preparedness and success had set in throughout the school, and staff and faculty waited anxiously for the results of the tests they had administered. Finally, the scores were released. The school had increased significantly. The hard work had paid off.

The secret to the school's success is a strategy of *concentrating on the mission and vision, the Big Picture*. Despite all the issues that came with the day-to-day running of a high school, the principal had never lost sight of the school's ultimate goal of raising students' test scores. Every time motivation sank lower, she held inspirational assemblies for the students and themed lunches for the teachers.

As civil rights leader Mahatma Gandhi once observed: "A small body of determined spirits fired by an unquenchable faith in their mission can alter the course of history."

The key to every goal is never to lose sight of this. A PLC is just such a "small body of determined spirits," one capable of attaining its goals (or altering the course of history) by concentrating on the Big Picture. The only condition is that they be fired by an unquenchable faith in their mission. Despite all the setbacks occurring during the year, the PLC must keep to a collective, unwavering course if it is to realize its goal.

Below are four actions to guide the activities while concentrating on the school's mission, vision, and Big Picture—all will strengthen the PLC.

Action 1: In order to get colleagues to care about the school's overall Big Picture you must learn to care about their contributions. Granted, you may or may not fully understand the content they teach, but you should recognize their contributions as members of the PLC. Everyone loves a little appreciation, so show interest in the content, ask questions, thank them for their efforts, tell them they did a fine job.

Action 2: Once your PLC members understand that you appreciate their Standpoints they will be more eager to participate in the mission and the vision-creating process. This is your opportunity to inspire colleagues and all stakeholders. It is really about defining the mission based on the collective vision of the PLC. You must not only inspire your colleagues, but also construct a clear Big Picture and forgo a rehashing of some vague statement from the past.

Action 3: It is equally important to obtain and to maintain member buy-in. After the development of the Big Picture, buy-in is liable to wear off quickly, like any novelty. Therefore, you must empower all PLC members to take ownership of the mission, vision, and Big Picture. Short of that, all of the cheerleading and coaching in the world would amount to little. At some point, the team needs to take the field and perform to the best of its ability.

Action 4: It is only human nature to translate a large, difficult, or long-term goal into more manageable subgoals. Completing limited subgoals tends to make everyone feel good. However, each completed task can compromise your motivation and progress toward the Big Picture. Too often people are so focused on the day-to-day activities and issues that the Big Picture gets lost.

Long-term goals render focus on the Big Picture more difficult. There will be times when the PLC fails or things don't turn out the way it is planned. When this happens, practice a strategy of *concentrating on the mission and vision and looking at the Big Picture.* As long as you stay on the yellow brick road, you are bound to reach the Emerald City.

STRUGGLE STRATEGY 5: FOCUS ON THE PROBLEM, NOT THE INDIVIDUAL

The May Day incident described in chapter 6 is a good example of how easy it is for the discourse to shift from the problem to the individual. In that incident, members met to discuss possible solutions to keep students from walking off campus in protest. With her single expression of concern the petite science teacher managed to set off a Struggle so significant that it stifled opinion for the remainder of the school year.

Sometimes an isolated statement can set into motion a Struggle among opposing views; sometimes it takes a clash of familiar Standpoints. Everyone has encountered at some point in the past at least one colleague who was labeled "problematic." *Focusing on the problem, not the individual,* will allow you to put aside your preconceived Standpoint about that colleague. He or she may not be the friendliest member of the group, or there may be a personality conflict, but this hardly means that the person as such has lost the legitimacy to raise an issue.

According to American professor of psychology Abraham Maslow, "If you only have a hammer, you tend to see every problem as a nail." He meant that all problems must be handled in a manner specific to its cause and nature. There is no "one size fits all" approach to dealing with problems relating to education. This is especially true when Standpoint directly contributes to the Struggle. You need a strategy for each problem.

Below are four actions to guide the discussion on the problem, instead of the individual, and to help you strengthen your PLC.

Action 1: Questions demand answers, which lead to more questions—this is what makes an investigative process. So be sure to identify and resolve the source of the Struggle. If you determine that a member is at fault, then try to correct that person's behavior. If you sense a legitimate issue, focus on that.

Action 2: Be patient and practice what you preach to your students. Refrain from making any judgment about a Struggle without taking the time to evaluate all the pertinent information. A hasty decision can do more harm than good if it proves incorrect. Keep the lines of communication open and allow colleagues to express their Standpoints. Then, separate objective information from subjective information to make the best decisions possible.

Action 3: Conversing with PLC colleagues is an important part of this exercise. Be direct and use clear language to explain the problem and its impact on the school with precision. Be sure, also, to separate objective from subjective information. This will allow everyone involved to recognize better your Standpoint and expectations. Beyond that try to speak in a manner that establishes member ownership and initiative with respect to problem resolution.

Action 4: Encourage colleagues to use "I" statements to identify and define the problem in hand. An "I" statement is a good way to assert one's own feelings or beliefs, unlike "You" statements, which draw attention to the other person. Ask each party to state openly what it deems the issue behind the Struggle to be. Concentrate on that issue and its possible solution without assigning fault or blame.

It is not hard to lose focus in a Struggle. A strategy *focused on the problem, not the individual,* will allow the members to inquire into the causes and to maintain a healthy dialogue. A PLC able to remove the element of blame and to work jointly toward solutions is clearly using member Standpoint to its advantage.

STRUGGLE STRATEGY 6: WORK THROUGH DIFFERENCES TO SOLVE PROBLEMS

All graduating seniors at a high school were required to complete a senior project. This yearlong task had three components: a career mentoring experience of twenty hours, a minimum eight-page written reflection of the mentee experience, and a visual presentation to summarize the experience. These components were the collaborative result of efforts undertaken by the school's leadership team. The important thing is that they neglected to designate individuals or departments to make sure the task was indeed completed. The leadership team then decided that twelfth-grade social science teachers were best qualified to monitor the mentoring experience, and that twelfth-grade English teachers should advise and grade the written assignments. The volunteering teachers would then attend and grade the student presentations.

Unfortunately, this did not go over well with the twelfth-grade teachers, and the leadership team that had created the task just slipped away without taking on extra responsibilities. Moreover, the twelfth-grade teachers felt slighted and unappreciated, since they were not consulted on the development of the senior project. Grudgingly, the twelfth-grade teachers—who were mandated the extra duties—worked to meet their responsibilities.

At the end of the year, when the time came for students to make their presentations, the volunteers were few and far between. The leadership team asked social science and English teachers if they were interested in attending the presentations. The teachers declined from frustration at how the whole situation had been handled. They pointed out their contributions and insisted it was only fair that others should do the same. After much discussion and compromise, it was decided the members of the leadership team, who had created the assignment in the first place, would sit in for all presenting seniors. The staff availed themselves of a *"work through differences to solve problems"* strategy for the benefit of students.

Famous American industrialist Henry Ford once said: "Coming together is a beginning; keeping together is progress; working together is success."

Throwing people together and telling them to get along on their own will not necessarily lead to compliance. There is bound to be a Struggle that tests the resiliency of the PLC. Members must have—or acquire—the skills to stay and work together toward their goals.

Below are four actions for working through differences, which means working past Struggle to strengthen the PLC.

Action 1: As we saw in the previous chapters, PLCs have diverse Standpoints, which we have no choice but to work with in order to find common ground. Members may disagree, but with time and attention colleagues should find more agreement on specific issues than disagreement. They have to determine what is *not* in dispute before looking for a lasting solution.

Action 2: Staff and faculty do not always get to pick the people they work with, which creates another condition for Struggle. They will have to agree to disagree on certain matters. Sometimes they just have to respect each other's Standpoint and move on. This is easier said than done, of course. But if everyone in the PLC is educated and experienced, why not respect one another's professional judgment regardless of the differences?

Action 3: "I" statements in communication can do wonders. They describe how their author feels but without blaming colleagues. Resolving a Struggle does not mean fighting to prove oneself right and colleagues wrong; rather, resolution implies coming to an agreement with which everyone in the PLC can be happy.

Action 4: Do you remember when your parents used to send you to your room for timeout to think about what you had done? This technique works on adults too. When you face a Struggle that needs resolving, take time out to reflect on the best way to deal with the problem, if possible. Responding in anger will only worsen the Struggle. Give yourself the time and space to permit levelheadedness to prevail. This way you will be able to work past differences and get to the main task: solving the problems at hand.

Setting goals is fine, but above all, PLC members need to learn the strategy of *working through differences to solve problems,* regardless of the internal Struggle that ensues, because their strength comes mainly from the diversity of Standpoints in the PLC. The sky is the limit once the members learn to work through their differences and concentrate on goal achievement.

STRUGGLE STRATEGY 7: SEEK AGREEMENT AND COMMUNICATE REASONING BEHIND DECISIONS

In the main there are three kinds of decisions. The first pertains to the leader who takes action alone, based on that person's official position or status in the organization. Face it, sometimes leaders have to arrive at a decision without input. This is the burden and responsibility that come with the office.

The second kind of decision is when the leader has no stake in the outcome and hands decision-making authority to the staff, which frequently means deciding on whatever suits them.

The third kind has to do with collective decisions that require input from staff.

These decisions define the leadership style of the administrator, and either increase or decrease the sense of empowerment and potential inside the PLC. The leader has to seek out input from the entire staff to arrive at a formula that elicits genuine commitment and engagement.

American physicist William Pollard noted, "Information is a source of learning. But unless it is organized, processed, and available to the right people in a format for decision making, it is a burden, not a benefit."

Clearly, he believed in the dissemination of information to as many members of the organization as possible, especially information regarding the decision-making process. An important step in making any type of decision is to communicate the reasoning behind the decision.

Action 1: If a unilateral decision must be made, you must still be able to explain your reasons behind that decision, and the best way to do it is in person. E-mails are an excellent medium of communication that circumvents the emotion and inflection of verbal exchange. Still, a great deal of misunderstanding can occur. People may not like the decision, but they will respect you for having enough respect to inform them in person and to accept the responsibility for the decision.

Action 2: A clearly defined decision-making process invites input from staff on issues that matter the most. The section on the fourth quadrant of the 4S Approach, Structure, has information about structuring devices and meeting designs to ensure higher levels of engagement. One caveat: this process should be undertaken in a staff or departmental meeting environment where all can judge on their own the input being recorded. After the meeting, transcribe the input onto a document and e-mail to all participants. Toward the end of this ongoing debate select a solution via this decision-making process. Recording and e-mailing to staff makes it difficult to argue over the engagement and the agreement on the decision.

The organization has to decide consensually what to do and then to execute the bulk of its work in the same spirit. Well-founded decisions, not to speak of easy communication among the members, can only strengthen the PLC. By the same token a strategy of continually *seeking agreement and communicating the reasoning behind those decisions* will dull the negative consequences of Struggle.

STRUGGLE STRATEGY 8: APOLOGIZE MEANINGFULLY

Apology is too tough a nut to crack for many people, whatever the issue. Nevertheless, *apologizing meaningfully* not only is a great way to deal with the Struggle, but also coheres well with Standpoint. The problem is when people expect an admission of guilt for some terrible wrong, not just a simple apology.

We have all made mistakes at one time or another. When it happens it is best to come clean and take ownership of our actions. However, *meaningful apology* is much more than having to admit to a wrongdoing. As the familiar saying goes, "Apologizing does not always mean you are wrong and the other person is right. It just means you value your relationship more than your ego."

Following through is, of course, another matter, perhaps because our sense of self tends to get in the way. When we struggle to see eye-to-eye, when we experience interpersonal conflict—due to our distinctive Standpoint—we tend to stand our ground. This is especially true when people feel passionate about the issue in hand.

A colleague of ours, Tracy Wilkins, once declared that passion plays a big role in group conversations. For one thing, it may steer people away from the very notion of apologizing to others. She added that "with that passion can come emotion. Emotion can override reason. It's not always easy, but you have to let others know you respect their ideas, even if you don't always agree." Whatever your motive or role in the matter, a simple apology can do wonders.

Below are four actions to guide your exchange during a meaningful apology, the goal being to strengthen relationships in your PLC.

Action 1: The next time disagreement erupts or someone's feelings get hurt—whether those of a colleague, boss, or someone you supervise—first try to understand what has led to the unease. Perhaps a decision was made and this individual had misgivings about the course of action, or some other thing had been said or done that might have provoked the ill feelings. Try walking in his or her shoes, so to speak; try to find out if you erred in entertaining the opposite view.

Action 2: Once you have a good idea about what led to the breakdown, extend your humble apology (even if you earnestly feel you have committed no wrong). This is simply to demonstrate that you value the relationship. If you stand on solid ground, then steer the apology toward the way they *feel* about the situation. You may even express regret for their *perception* of the situation. Let the person know how much you appreciate his or her willingness to share a concern openly with you. They could have refrained from speaking at all, allowing the issue to fester and causing even deeper resentment. By the same token, they at least adhered to the first strategy of this chapter: *Be honest and transparent, however difficult the conversation may be.* Keep in mind, too, that your apology has to be sincere. Others will have no trouble seeing through an artificial apology.

Action 3: Should an action, inaction, or interaction on your part—right or wrong—lead to frayed emotions, ask how the grief can be avoided the next time a similar situation arises. There is a good chance the subject will come up on the heels of your apology. If it doesn't, then go ahead and ask. If you cannot adhere to their position, then make your intentions crystal clear and give your word that you will do your best to do right the next time.

Action 4: If the negative circumstances recur, do your best to follow through with whatever vow you have given. Following through with any commitment whatsoever tends to convey trust and speaks volumes about your devotion to existing relationships. Anything short of that will either erode trust or kill it at the drop of a hat.

Apologies do not have to take place only in one-on-one meetings or between only two individuals. By way of example, a principal and her administrative team decided that, based on test score data, teachers would incorporate a particular practice into their daily lessons. Unsurprisingly, a handful of teachers were upset at the decision, arguing they were denied a chance to chime in their two cents' worth in the decision making. The principal responded with a bold step.

At the next staff meeting she stood up in front of the whole staff and declared: "Everyone, I am truly sorry for making such a major school-wide decision without seeking your input first. It completely strays from our vision of collaboration. Each and every one of you has great ideas and I should have listened before taking action. We are going to still move forward with the decision, and I can assure you that in the future you will be a part of the process. Again, I'm sorry!"

Her decision may well have been a good one, but the path to it should have involved more people.

Later that day a new teacher thanked her for apologizing and remarked how much courage it must have taken to apologize in front to everyone. "I've worked at many different schools," he added, "and have never had a principal apologize out loud like that. Thank you." Although the original decision stood, the principal had all but acknowledged the importance of her relationship with the staff. A simple "sorry" goes a long way to communicating to others at least your willingness to listen to what they have to say. Ease of communication is vital to any healthy relationship. Arguing your own point of view uncompromisingly will only increase the general level of stress and anger.

Employing a strategy of *apologizing meaningfully* should earn your expressions of regret two words in reply: "Apology accepted." Even if no one uttered these words, the verbal and nonverbal communications alone are liable to communicate acceptance.

There will be times, though, when your sincerity fails to sway the general sentiment, because either the person or group is simply unprepared to accept your apology. This would reflect their Standpoint on the issue. Should their Standpoint get in the way of agreement, maintain your apologetic attitude, follow through with your commitments, and let time heal any wounds.

III

Solidarity

> The function of the PLC is teamwork, in the simplest sense. . . . It is collaboration at its finest.
> —Paula Sorensen, principal, Salt Lake City, UT

This section on the third S in the 4S Approach elucidates the importance of building effective PLC teams. Differing Standpoints lead to Struggle. But when Struggle has been overcome the new focus is on unification: namely, Solidarity.

Solidarity connotes the coming together of a team, only more strongly than before its advent. The source of a team's strength is a function of Solidarity's power. This power can be pivotal as the members move from a loose collection of individuals concerned with a single task to complex, highly functional teams working interdependently to accomplish overarching school-wide goals. The latter are the driving force behind the PLC model. Without relentless, concentrated teamwork a school has little hope of reaching its fullest potential. Teams are foundational in this sense.

It is important to consider Solidarity in relation to the other two quadrants, Standpoint and Struggle. Their interaction should not be stymied. Whenever diverse individuals come together on a set of tough issues, armed with a team perspective, Standpoint has to be taken into consideration. The differences that arise will naturally lead to Struggle; teams have to be able to work through those differences to reconnect and reinvigorate the organization with a view to deepening the synergy. This is the essence of Solidarity—a union that spells organizational triumph.

In the next three chapters, we expand on the development and preservation of Solidarity in the school. This teamwork builds "power." Chapter 9 ("Room Numbers") introduces the idea of Solidarity and its connection to effective teams. The following chapter ("The Four Key Foundations") establishes a framework for building teams in a school environment. Lastly, chapter 11 ("Strategies for Solidarity") highlights eight distinct practices that move Solidarity from theory to individual practice to shared school-wide culture.

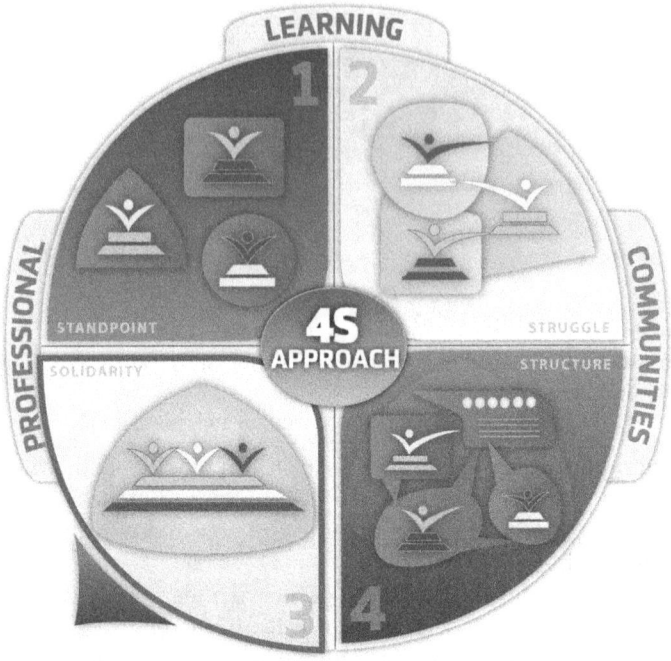

Figure 8.3. The 4S Approach—Solidarity

If you strive to achieve the *community* in PLC, then pay close attention to Solidarity. It's just another way of spelling your commitment and engagement as team leader.

NINE
Room Numbers

> As a result of the PLC, student progress will increase, learning gaps will decrease, and learning will become student-centered (even fun!).
> —Jillian Laute, student teacher

Picture a new vice principal sitting in the principal's office discussing his future. During the conversation an odd feeling of wonder mixed with confusion overcomes him. A few months earlier, he was groping for a way to connect with staff and break through the negative stereotyping, from which administrations just like his have been ailing around the country. Things are looking up.

He turns to the principal. "Katie, I feel like the staff is looking at me differently," he says, almost in a self-edifying tone. "Things feel different. It's like I can talk to them now. What is the difference?" It seems people are both listening to and accepting his ideas more often, and plainly enjoying conversing with him.

"It's pretty simple. You showed them you understood what was important to them . . . did something about it and in turn made their lives a bit easier. You showed them you wanted to work together."

Her response struck the new vice principal. It was, he thought, wonderfully penetrating and so utterly confusing! So he thinks some more: How on earth did he manage to pull off this tremendous feat? He has absolutely no inkling.

Trying not to sound like a complete ignoramus, he assumes a more serious tone. "Did any of the teachers give you specifics on what made the difference? I'd like to build on that success."

No sooner have the words left his mouth than he realizes his folly. The principal looks at him with a chuckle, having realized the man has absolutely no idea that his deeds helped him gain the confidence of staff. "The room numbers," she tells him.

A light bulb lit inside his head. When the new school was built the contractors had installed beautiful signs on every classroom door and entrance. They were grey plastic outlined in dark blue with raised letters; they also had Braille so every student could use them. Each door and entrance was beautifully marked for easy access. The only thing the contractors failed to do was anticipate the behavior of the students.

Everybody has his opinion on the unpredictability and occasionally destructive behavior of adolescents. The first thing the students figured out about the signage at their school was how easy it was to scrape off the letters on the signs. They did a job on the *C*s and *L*s, leaving "assroom" in plain view. And the joke was on. For two years the topic of signs kept cropping up—arguments back and forth between the district and contractors about whom to blame. All the while the teachers continued working in their "assrooms," frustrated by the inaction.

At the start of the second year of arguments the new vice principal, motivated by a wider need to improve the school, decided to take action on the signs. He approached the principal and asked for $250 to buy address number signs for each classroom at the nearest hardware store. It took two days but he installed a room number for every single classroom door. Finally, the teachers that August entered #805 or 807, not "Assroom #805."

Unwittingly, the vice principal had stumbled on the one thing that made a psychological difference to the teachers more than anything else. Imagine the relief!

WHAT IS SOLIDARITY?

The above anecdote illustrates one manner of bringing staff together. Just the feeling of coming together can have a transforming effect on the school culture. When the staff members understand their interconnections and value each other, there is no limit to what they can achieve. Let us for a moment consider Solidarity through its most elementary properties, much like any other kind of relationship characterized by conflict.

Conflict may suggest a wider Struggle. To a husband and wife it may amount to nothing more than a good old-fashioned fight. Sometimes, though, the spouses' sense of awareness shrinks down to negative thoughts about each other. The husband might think, "Why did I marry this stubborn, headstrong, self-centered woman?" While the wife might be muttering to herself, "Who are we kidding?" before dressing him down for being hardheaded, judgmental, and just an all-around bag of wind! The fight rages on, punctuated with angry stares.

Then, a corner of the woman's mouth turns up slightly, and the anger dissipates as quickly as it came. A different feeling emerges after that—a flash of love, forgiveness, understanding, warmth. The couple makes up, hugs and kisses. There is reuniting and reconnecting, not to mention the reinvigoration of the relationship after the Struggle—now that is Solidarity!

This is precisely the sort of Solidarity that school staff ought to have for each other. It makes everything possible. It is not as if Solidarity were some obscure and unstudied notion; on the contrary, it is grounded in theory. The challenge for planners is to take it into consideration, press the available research into service, and design an innovative and caring academic environment in which all the students can give their best. Clearly, such a transformation presupposes good interaction among the adults. Meetings, meeting rooms, and meeting agendas do little, on their own, to heighten their caring or to deal with questions of innovation and the members' high expectations. All these factors should be used to improve the effectiveness of the team.

UNDERSTANDING WHAT IS IMPORTANT

Diverse Standpoints may lead individual members to value things differently, but educators who come together must set their hearts on identifying a core set of values they can share. Every human being possesses a core set of values; the Struggle begins when at least one person in the group does not value the same things as another. Understanding what things are most important to the school, though, should pave the way to more effective teamwork. For that, the teams need continually to evaluate each other's Standpoints, because Standpoints change over time. This too gives certain inevitability to Struggle.

The first step toward Solidarity is to understand the needs and values that lie just below the surface. Indeed, the primary purpose for coming together is to take stock of what the members value most. In a group setting, purpose should have the following three characteristics: common identity and tenets, common tasks, and a sense of potency (Harvey & Drolet, 2004). These characteristics shed light on both why people coalesce into groups and the very *purpose* of their collective work.

A healthy sense of potency, in particular, begets a "can-do" attitude. The most successful teams are deeply convinced of their ability to ensure student learning. Teams that feel capable in this respect tend to act more cohesively than teams that do not.

Henry Ford's insight into potency and success is fitting. "Whether you think you can or think you can't, you are right," he said.

FINDING COMMON GROUND

Understanding shared values should move the PLC members to a point where their differences lead to a point of intersection. Dig deep enough and you will discover just how much others share in the things you claim to hold dear. Value differences merely account for the Struggle; to move forward you must also fathom the extent to which your group members are alike in respect of those values.

By themselves the values shared by the members may not lessen the contest of competing needs, but identifying common needs can only render the Struggle a decidedly less petty affair. Distinguishing the Struggle from the need or the value perspective allows for both disagreement and trust. This is important, as the trust you build up through Struggle is the mainstay of Solidarity in a PLC—a cornerstone for your team. If team members distrust each other, there is no team. Without trust there is only a collection of individuals cohabitating under a vacuous name.

Trust has five properties: interdependence, consistency, honesty, affability, and extension. Cultivating these properties helps create and perpetuate the relationships that make up a team, not just a loose group. Team members who enjoy strong relationships work as colleagues, but the team itself will not flourish alone, in a vacuum. Relationship building aims at moving teams to ever-higher levels of effectiveness. As useful as all the mixers, parties, and potlucks may be for teambuilding devices, far more important in the end is the fulfillment of practical tasks.

Relationships built on trust provide the glue that holds a team together from conflict to conflict, as long as one remembers that Struggle is necessary for success. Struggle reflects the tension between the novelty of fresh ideas and the inertia of the present. Remove this tension and you will compromise your organization's growth and progress, without which of course no amount of teamwork will adapt your PLC to the fast-changing social landscape. That is not to say that conflict will never be a destructive force. But then, a little destruction can make for a lot of valuable growth.

In short, your ability to think of conflict as a healthy part of the growing process is the hallmark of effective teams. As the saying goes, you can't reach your destination if you don't leave the spot you're standing on.

Be Willing to Give a Little

It is worth repeating: *You can't reach your destination if you don't leave the spot you're standing on.* In a conflict setting this piece of wisdom implies compromise. Solidarity can only take root if common ground is found, needs are understood, and teammates compromise for the good of the team. Compromise cannot happen without the will to give in a little on one's position. Truly effective teams are those whose members must be willing to yield in the interest of a true win-win situation.

It all comes down to the following: team-member interaction must exemplify caring, community, and flexibility. The world is changing apace. "This means that, while specific future developments are increasingly difficult to predict, we can make two predictions with great certainty: The pace of change will continue to increase and interdependence will continue to grow" (Joiner & Josephs, 2007, p. 5).

The fact is that schools have to service an ever-diversifying student body, and the changing dynamics are bringing new needs to the fore. PLCs must find the means to identify and deal with the most important of those needs, to work toward common goals, and to compromise, if students are to derive the benefits they deserve from modern education.

Either our schools place themselves on the edge of change or they will quickly grow obsolete. Compromise and change are other instruments that teams can use to adapt to the complexity of our world. Adapt, improvise, and overcome.

In the end, the refusal to compromise is symptomatic of creeping stagnation.

COME TOGETHER AGAIN

Solidarity is more than just a word or idea—it entails feelings of togetherness, commitment to one another, and renewed strength. And compromise solidifies it by, as we discovered from the anecdote in this chapter, helping renew the two disputing colleagues' sense of connection. This "renewal" can manifest itself overtly. For example, a husband hugs and kisses his wife. PLC members may make light of reinvigorated feelings of closeness and camaraderie, but coming together after compromise signals the unmistakable presence of Solidarity.

TEN
The Four Key Foundations

> A professional learning community is the way a school community works collaboratively to meet the needs of all students.
> —Dr. Susan Steaffens, principal, Las Vegas, NV

Much ink has been spilled about effective teams, but all the theorizing in the world will not make a team more effective. It takes deliberate, honest, and committed *action* to create both the conditions for effectiveness and the team Solidarity on which it depends, since Solidarity represents the culmination of the team spirit. In the words of Ralph Waldo Emerson, "An ounce of action is worth a ton of theory."

Briefly, the Four Key Foundations (figure 10.1) enable PLC members to develop effective teams by utilizing their school's "capacity":

- Foundation #1: Listening to People and the Environment
- Foundation #2: Building Agreements
- Foundation #3: Co-creating Purpose
- Foundation #4: Fostering Effective Teams

Although this chapter discusses each foundation separately, they are interconnected and hierarchical. First introduced in Wiseman's *Strong Schools, Strong Leaders* (2010), these foundations resemble a road map for higher levels of team achievement and are key to reinforcing Solidarity in the 4S Approach. Richter (2012) has examined significant evidence that points to differences between high- and low-achieving schools. His conclusions show that high-achieving schools possessed statistically higher means or capacity in relation to the four foundations. This is the evidentiary context within which we advance our ideas here.

Figure 10.1. The Four Key Foundations

FOUNDATION 1: LISTENING TO PEOPLE AND THE ENVIRONMENT

Schools embody myriad experiences, opinions, and perspectives of unique individuals. From this perspective, Standpoint stands supreme. As an approach, consequently, listening to people and the environment encourages principals and teachers to find ways to seek and recognize a host of ideas, good and bad, percolating right in their midst. This is about sparking genuine commitment, rather than perfunctory compliance, in order to tap into the collective intelligence of the school.

Listening to People

Listening to people? Nothing could be simpler, you may say. After all, to find out what is going on in your school, you have only to listen to people. Granted, each school has its unique culture, range of skills, and basic disposition. Yet why can there not be a single method for intervening or enriching a school's curriculum? And why does a curriculum that worked wonderfully, say, in a large urban school in Chicago fail in a rural district of Northern California?

Don't wait for a silver bullet, much less a one-size-fits-all method of approach. Ideas may work in several schools or teams but not necessarily all. Why not? Because they take root and grow in a unique context proper to a living group, not a theoretical one. Unfortunately, ideas cannot simply be doled out like so many plug-and-play solutions. One must understand the strengths, weaknesses, concerns, hopes, passions, and goals of the staff. New programs frequently fail through no fault of the curriculum, which may well be outstanding; only, the members are simply not listening to one another.

Here is an apt question you should ask yourself: How often do you make a decision based on what someone tells you about a situation rather than on what the participants themselves say?

Take political elections, for instance. People make judgments based partly on aired interviews and panel debates with the candidates—it is part of the ritual. Some people will be scandalized if a candidate's personal indiscretions come to light. But how many of us take the trouble to question the candidate before judging the veracity of the allegations? The same happens—albeit on a smaller scale—when Standpoints clash and grievances are vented in a school. Fortunately, principals and teachers have the choice to act in a more inclusive, responsible, and positive manner, without the least regard to public polls or popularity.

True listening is an active process, where PLC members have to take active steps to solicit information. One-on-one conversations, small group interviews, and staff surveys must be the norm even in large institutions, where such interaction tends to be rare. We should not be surprised if PLCs that fail to listen actively lose support and fall apart.

Pay Attention to the Environment

At any given school, staff and faculty are always ready to put a spin on how they go about their work because they think this will foster positive attitudes about them. Like everyone else they want to feel acknowledged and respected. They are more inclined to get involved and do what they can to make a solution work if they are included, valued, and listened to. Listening is the first step toward such inclusion. The second is taking time out to reflect on what was said. Stepping out on the balcony may allow the members to look at the big picture and consider the veracity of the information they gathered from their conversations with fellow members.

By way of example, I have had to teach my class about geometric proofs using a classic T-chart approach to organize their thinking. This is because, from the outset, they would get so caught up in their reasons and statements that they ended up forgetting what it was they were trying to prove. I have to keep reminding them to stop writing statements and reasons and to think about the proof. Stop and draw a picture, I say.

The same thing can happen inside school administrations, faculties, and staff purporting to base themselves on the PLC model. As a team and organization, stop from time to time and go to the balcony. Think of the big picture. What are you trying to accomplish? How do all the conversations, curriculum, ideas, and plans you have had fit together?

What's the Purpose?

School leaders and staff routinely make assumptions about the intentions of the people around them. However, assumptions are a rather precarious plank to be standing on. The only way to assess the intentions of others is to listen, reflect, and, if necessary, step back—in short, as DuFour et al. (2004) put it, to understand the fundamental purpose for our existence is equally to create and maintain a viable PLC.

Moreover, why we are here—our "fundamental purpose"—has to be broached openly. We readily assume why we are all here, as a group, but group divisions can easily manifest themselves even at this most basic level, if the range of opinions fails to add up to a common stance. Are we here to provide opportunity for students? Are we here to encourage students to do their best? Are we here to ensure students learn at high levels? These questions need to be considered through the prism of individuals and that of the unique environment of each school.

So reflect on the conversations taking place within your school environment until the purpose of each member of the administration, faculty, and staff is crystal clear and understood all around. Take a listen to the people and to the Structure already in place. It may reveal that this conversation is long overdue, and you may find a few surprises along the way. In my experience, some of the biggest professional Struggles usually revolve around coming to terms with fellow educators whose fundamental purpose is different from mine. It goes without saying, but the bigger issue here is that the difference between spotting an opportunity for improvement and raising the overall level of learning may pale in comparison with ideological chasm dividing the members.

Shared Decision Making

Shared decision making, which figures prominently in much of the literature in this area of research, is part and parcel of listening to the environment. The evidence shows overwhelmingly that school or department leaders benefit from a richer source of information and loyalty when they listen to colleagues before arriving at a decision than if they disregard input from others. The input of colleagues underpins "teamness."

But shared decision making and listening to the environment are also very broad terms. To be useful to PLC practitioners, they have to be operationalized. Hord (2004) argued that shared decision making—one of her Five Dimensions of PLC—"requires collegial and facilitative participation of the principal who shares leadership—and thus, power and authority—by inviting staff input and action in decision-making" (p. 7). However, leaders are not just in the business of receiving input; they must actively seek it from their staff, a drawn-out process that begins with listening.

A good leader actively listens from within both the context of local human interactions and the wider organization. This makes active listening a kind of pervasive process of reciprocation whereby the members endeavor to build meaning together. Here, the leader has to do his or her utmost to make the sharing of possibly sensitive information safe by seeking to understand before demanding to be understood.

How well leaders listen is partly reflected in their readiness to act upon the information received. Failing to act on information requiring action is to ignore it. The literature on PLCs has identified action as data or information driven. The use of data gathered either from observation or through staff conversations offers essentially what listening to the environment does. Here too, obviously, data is crucial to planning, collaboration, and decision making in schools (Marzano, 2005).

Listening to the environment encapsulates the leader's understanding of the environment. Not only that, but the resulting transparency in decision making fosters mutual trust, not just a better appreciation of the inner workings of the environment. Hidden agendas and underlying power structures easily undermine honesty in staff relations. Allowing colleagues to defend their interests and express their passion for the work they do, on the other hand, will create a whole new set of environmental conditions.

Shared Responsibility for Decisions

Sharing the responsibility for decisions and accepting those decisions is indispensable to team effectiveness. Decision making can be a messy process at the best of times, and unanimity is simply a myth. Since there will always be disagreement, it rests on the members to deal positively with it and to recognize the will of the group as a whole—short of external arbitration, no one else will do it for them. This partly means standing behind the group decision once it is taken. This is the hallmark of effectiveness.

Sharing responsibility suggests that the PLC is doing more than simply voting on the options put forward. Letting people advance their ideas presupposes a healthy sense of responsibility and a level of commitment to the process. Moreover, the time allotted for decision making must be *perceived* to be as important and not just another opportunity for airing complaints or hobnobbing casually over coffee and pastries.

Consensus on Decisions

Consensus provides the path by which decisions translate into action in the real world of effective teams. Ideally, it indicates that the will of the group has been understood, accepted, and slated for implementation by all the members, inclusively (DuFour, 2006). That said, it may happen that the team members fail to agree on a course of action. Yet merely to acknowledge the general will confirms that the members have linked shared decision making with shared responsibility for the decisions. This link demands commitment to the consensus, which itself demonstrates how willing the school or department leader is to listen to the environment and the staff.

The 4S Approach to reviving PLCs is about loops of thinking and learning, much like a process within a process.

Step out onto the balcony and you will see the big picture. The first of the Four Key Foundations—listening to people and the environment—comprises the initial step toward building effective teams. It can only occur at the team level. At the school level, it assumes the form of a Standpoint. It is absolutely critical to the health of a PLC that the Standpoint of the faculty and staff not only be clearly understood and communicated, but also acknowledged and valued. The eight Standpoint Strategies empower the PLC to create a functioning organization and to work for successful outcomes for the students.

FOUNDATION 2: BUILDING AGREEMENTS

Building agreements has a lot to do with organizational learning. Once the leader has listened to environment, the faculty and staff will be better prepared to come to a common understanding on the modalities of working together. Agreement, when reached, is a manifestation of this consensus-building effort (DuFour, 2006; Wiseman, 2010). Past research has consistently identified consensus as a practice that not only gains school leaders "instructional momentum," but also enhances the motivational level of teachers (McLaughlin & Talbert, 2001; Rosenholtz, 1989). Building agreements cannot take place without a level of member interaction that promotes shared information, trust, and open but direct communication.

Handle Open Direct Conflict with Respect

Expect Struggle, or conflict, in practically every kind of social group. Groups without conflict are groups without consequence. Movement engenders Struggle, irrespective of direction. To progress—a kind of movement—means having conflict. Why? Because conflict is a sign of health in an organization, as long as it has not reached a toxic level. Therefore, handling conflict openly and directly should not be underestimated.

Hidden agendas, parking-lot conversations, and power also "move," but too often they move behind closed doors, and that is the trouble. On the other hand, openness and directness in conflict among staff allow for an authentic exchange of ideas to take place. Building Agreements stands on a process we have called Listening to the Environment, the first foundation. It brings out the underlying thoughts and feelings of faculty and staff even against a background of conflict.

In general, close-mindedness and circuitous communication stifle listening and communication. Somehow Solidarity has to come about in a manner that enables the participants to emerge from Struggle with a new unified understanding of Standpoint for all the PLC members.

In sum, failing to deal with conflict openly and directly can result in equally toxic relationships as those of a conflict too destructive to be of use to anyone. How the members treat one another affects agreements, either furthering or hindering Solidarity on the team. Differences of opinions and open conflict must be handled in a way that preserves the dignity of all members. Struggle should never be allowed to trigger anxiety, animosity, and humiliation, which only destroy trust and understanding among members. Showing respect during a conflict is essential to keeping teams effective.

Norms and Guidelines for Group Interaction

The second key foundation, Building Agreements, is grounded in the interaction of effective teams, norms, and guidelines for behaviors that establish positive working relationships among members. The norms and guidelines for interaction must inculcate a sense of accountability that all share. PLC members have to be ready to hold each other to them, as well as to share in the responsibility of creating them.

Shared accountability is the natural extension of shared decision making. With respect to the first key foundation, we regard the idea of shared decision making and responsibility as part of listening to the environment, and sharing in decision making as sharing the accountability for and to the decision reached.

Building agreements improves Solidarity among teams, as Richter's study (2012) shows. He determined that the second key foundation of Building Agreements was statistically higher in schools with higher levels of achievement than in schools with lower levels of achievement. In both high- and low-achieving schools, however, Building Agreements exhibited the lowest score of the Four Key Foundations. Richter argues that the factor limiting school success might be the level at which members reach and then adhere to a given agreement. To build a successful and effective PLC one must improve Solidarity through the creation, communication, and enforcement of agreements among team members.

FOUNDATION 3: CO-CREATING PURPOSE

The co-creation of purpose, the third foundation, refers to the sharing of a common vision and mission. Such a vision will not materialize in a single stroke. Sometimes it has to grow through continual discussion and debate. By collaborating and dialoguing critically about purpose and meaning, a school will find its purpose, one that all its members will somehow share. This purposefulness will breathe life into your organization, guiding your day-to-day activities (DuFour, 2008; Schmoker, 2006).

Co-creating purpose will fill your need to define and agree upon both the fundamental purpose for coming together and the guiding principles for normal interactions with students and parents. It has to do with the small stuff no less than with the big picture.

Connecting Personal Passions with Organizational Vision

This is about connecting people to the vision of an organization with the aim of co-creating purpose. Members of true PLCs know in their heart of hearts that their mission and vision statements have to be more than just cleverly crafted sentences. Both should inspire without losing their edge of realism. With the advent of a common understanding about what the members are thinking (while listening to the environment) and about the guidelines for acceptable interaction (while building agreements), the connection will fall naturally in place across the organization.

Above all, the purpose for coming together and dedicating oneself to the work must be found. Here, professional goals alone will not suffice—they reflect little more than a superficial commitment to the vision and mission.

Luckily, organization members bring passions to their jobs. These passions are a special resource and may be aligned with the organization's vision and mission to maximize the results. Personal passions intersect with organizational mission in a zone of maximum potentiality. Whereas listening to the environment helps identify this zone, just as building agreement advances the members' ongoing conversation, co-creating purpose specifically unifies the personal and professional traits of each employee within the organization.

FOUNDATION 4: FOSTERING EFFECTIVE TEAMS

Schools need this last foundation for effective teamwork, the quality of which easily predicts the effectiveness of the school (Richter, 2012). Face it: effective teams are the bedrock of the organization, so much so that PLCs may be considered the very manifestation of effective school teams. The majority of research sees the connection, making it harder to ignore its relevance to school success (DuFour, 1998; Fullan, 1991; Rosenholtz, 1989; Wiseman, 2008, 2010).

Camaraderie

As we have argued, relationships are critical to the success of an organization. Camaraderie builds upon co-creating purpose and, more specifically, the tacit recognition and celebration of success. Building those relationships and acquiring a sense of unity among the group can prolong the "celebration," as it were. When combined with a common vision, shared responsibility to the team, and sense of trust camaraderie can generate the requisite energy to develop an effective work environment.

Process Checks and Group Maintenance

Periodic group reflections have the advantage of firming up team effectiveness. As "checks," they permit the members to evaluate the effectiveness of the current process. The fact is that good working teams always make time to evaluate their structure and organization. Groups that engage in regular time-out or maintenance sessions to address individual concerns about processes or behaviors ensure the productive behavior of their group.

High-Performing Teams

It is not hard to overlook the developmental character of the Four Key Foundations. For peak PLC performance, each foundation basically has to build on the previous one, working honestly through conflict for genuine solutions. Such solutions require high-level discourse, which—when properly based on asking and listening—is an excellent way to disseminate information to all the members of the PLC and for creating a common frame of reference.

Before even thinking of organizational flexibility, however, the members should encourage risk taking and tolerate a certain level of error, both of which may be considered opportunities for growth in high-performing teams. Safety and trust must be felt among the members of the group; this is what, in turn, will allow them to live with minimal error as an opportunity for growth.

Finally, the fourth foundation exhibits conceptual overlap with both other foundations and the preceding discussion on the 4S Approach, Standpoint, Struggle, and Solidarity.

ELEVEN
Strategies for Solidarity

> The outcomes of the PLC are to identify needs among students, share effective practices and monitor progress. This approach represents a shift from isolated planning to team planning and depends on an open, trusting and fully committed culture of learning in the school.
> —Dr. Dan Mass, chief information officer, Littleton, CO

Teamwork is the engine of the PLC. Its most outstanding strategies require members to

1. Accept different ways of accomplishing tasks, and encourage risk taking.
2. Build team agreements that further support school-wide agreements.
3. Support the greater good, rather than individual interests.
4. Regularly attend to group maintenance and processes.
5. Use a team-survey instrument to develop teamwork and unity.
6. Incorporate individual goals and passions into the organizational mission and vision.
7. Celebrate personal and professional successes.
8. Enjoy food and play together.

SOLIDARITY STRATEGY 1: ACCEPT DIFFERENT WAYS OF ACCOMPLISHING TASKS, AND ENCOURAGE RISK TAKING

As a mathematics teacher, I found that students love to inquire into the right method to solve a particular problem. So I make a point of encouraging them to explore different avenues that seem to point to a solution. When I asked them, "How do you get to the supermarket?" hands quick-

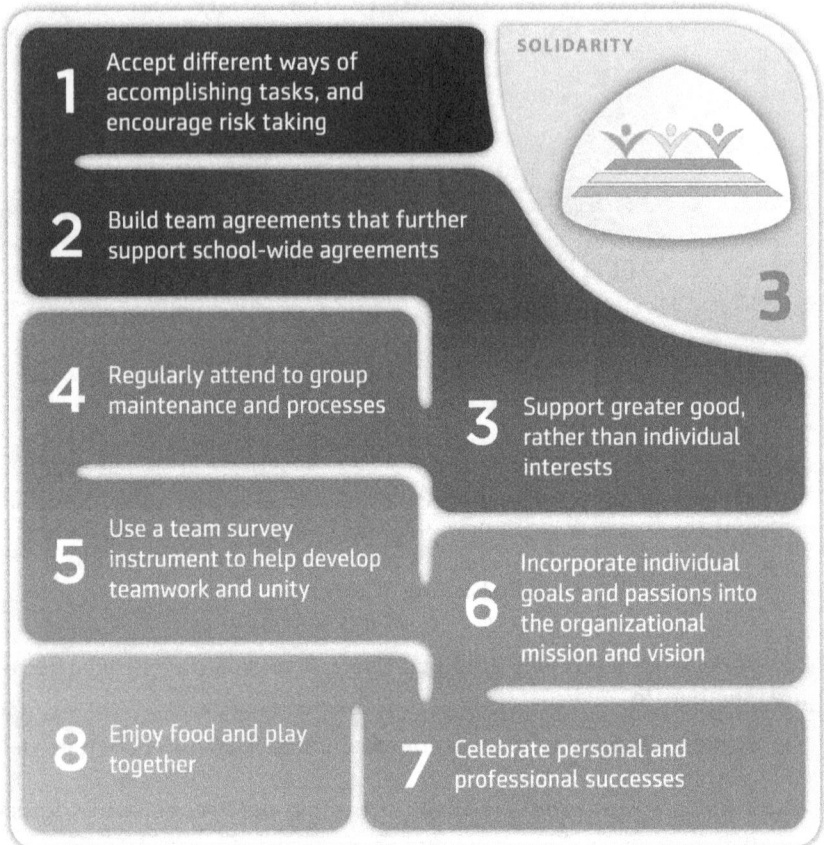

Figure 11.1. Eight Strategies for Solidarity

ly rose around the room, and they managed to come up with dozens of different solutions. They could get there by car, bus, bicycle, or walking.

Then I asked, "Which of these solutions offers the right way to get to the supermarket?" Their response? They're all good.

Thomas A. Edison, American inventor and businessman, noted, "Being busy does not always mean real work. The object of all work is production or accomplishment and to either of these ends there must be forethought, system, planning, intelligence, and honest purpose, as well as perspiration. Seeming to do is not doing."

Edison was thinking of the importance of keeping busy vs. accomplishing a task. Instead, many PLC leaders waste time and effort trying to mold colleagues into their image. Their energies could be better spent pursuing organizational goals. All PLC members need to understand and apply this lesson, because each member has a determinate set of skills and expertise that grow over time. But sometimes expertise gets in the way.

Rather than try to reshape it just to conform to a leader's narrow individual view of how to accomplish a particular task, the group should step back and allow its members to draw up their solution. In the end, the results will speak for themselves.

Action 1: The next time your group plans an activity or strategy, why not allow staff to take full responsibility for it? Set the parameters and adopt a means to check on progress. Make sure staff is not being set up for a fall, but allow for small bumps in the road along the way. Risk taking goes hand in hand with tolerance of error. What plan of action your staff draws up may well differ from what the leader might come up with.

Since it is the teachers who will execute the work, however, the staff's output has to be meaningful to them. In turn, the staff need to align with their own personal and professional goals. Doing so allows them to choose how they work and pursue their tasks, giving way to higher levels of commitment to the projected outcome.

As much as professionals would like to come together to develop a plan of action that leads to positive outcomes, this is not always possible in practice. A modest plan can make a huge difference by either increasing or destroying Solidarity. The fact is that the first attempt at change will look nothing like the successful program implemented, once the cycle of "data analysis and implementation of new ideas" has reached its limit.

Action 2: Recognize and commend staff when they arrive at a plan of action, even if the prospects for success seem low. In the event of mistakes, it is important to maintain the planners in their present positions. Removing people from decision-making positions at the slightest error rapidly conveys a sense of intolerance. Better to give decision makers another opportunity and to coach them. By accepting the possibility of errors, on the other hand, PLC colleagues encourage healthy risk taking. This agrees with their interest, since change will not occur without some risk taking. Besides, errors will occur whatever the path or pace of improvement. Far more important is for the improvement simply to happen.

Embracing a strategy of *accepting different ways of accomplishing tasks and encouraging risk taking* will demonstrate faith in the abilities of your colleagues. So encourage Solidarity by according staff the right to commit errors as they search for ways to accomplish their tasks.

SOLIDARITY STRATEGY 2: BUILD TEAM AGREEMENTS THAT FURTHER SUPPORT SCHOOL-WIDE AGREEMENTS

This strategy goes hand in hand with Struggle Strategy 3, which relates to school-wide agreement and the addressing of past conflict. Same idea here, but on a smaller scale: team members meet regularly to develop commitments to expected individual and team behavior. *School-wide* agreements may be more wide-ranging, but *team* agreements pertain to the individual members and the challenges facing the team. Teams display a much deeper sense of togetherness and intimacy.

As British Labour Party politician David Blunkett put it, "Strengthening our identity is one way of reinforcing people's confidence and sense of citizenship and well-being."

Yes, a school can exist as a PLC; however, the building, meeting time, place, even the name do not exhaust what a PLC should be. Rather, each member's commitment to the goals and processes determines its success. The individual is paramount here, just as *valuing the ideas of others*, by extension, is necessary for team effectiveness.

A team's deeper commitment around a particular agreement might be expressed as follows: "Before a team decision is reached each member will have the chance to share his or her ideas on the topic. Everyone's ideas will be considered." This provides a clearer picture of expected behavior.

Action 1: Each team's first action is to evaluate personal fulfillment in a given school-wide agreement—that is, with regard to each team's success in following through with an established agreement. One technique is for each team member to rate the team's adherence to the school-wide agreement using a simple five-point Likert scale—5 ("Very Successful"), 4 ("Successful"), 3 ("Neutral"), 2 ("Unsuccessful"), and 1 ("Very Unsuccessful"). That member will then share his score on each item and explain the attendant thought processes.

Action 2: Once everyone has had the opportunity to share his or her ratings aloud, the team may then calculate the pooled average for each item (or agreement). For instance, if a four-member team had scores of 3, 4, 4, and 2 on a particular agreement, then the average would be 3.25. The group has to rank all the items based on their averages, hopefully for results they could celebrate.

Action 3: After listing each agreement by average, from highest to lowest, one has to step back, observe, and rejoice at those items perceived by the team as being strong points. Commit to the continuous development and enhancement of team strengths.

Action 4: After the celebration, it's time to work on agreements that yield the lowest means. At this point, the team must explain what the low-scoring agreements signify to the team. How does the group, whether as a whole or as individuals, overcome the challenges? What added commitments can be made to improve these areas? Put pen to paper—*build team agreements that further support school-wide agreements.*

Action 5: Adhere to the agreements, hold one another accountable for the agreements, re-form and revisit agreements whenever necessary.

SOLIDARITY STRATEGY 3: SUPPORT GREATER GOOD, RATHER THAN INDIVIDUAL INTERESTS

Like others in the field, the authors of this book hardly chose education as a career to strike it rich or to find fame. Working with students can satisfy the desire to help people find achievement through education, which in the end of course inspires and shapes our future leaders. Some love working in education because they have a passion for learning and the pursuit of knowledge.

Whatever the reason for entering this honorable profession, service to others is central to a healthy Standpoint. As a strategy, *supporting the greater good rather than individual interests* is a good way to keep Standpoint alive inside ourselves as we contribute to the Solidarity of our PLC.

According to famous NFL coach Vince Lombardi, "Individual commitment to a group effort—that is what makes a team work, a company work, a society work, a civilization work."

True, no one can go it alone. It takes a genuine effort—on the part of all the members—for a school to realize its goals, whereby the individual chooses to commit to and support the greater good. Embarking on this makes the PLC members far stronger and capable of success.

Below are four actions in support of the greater good, which should result in a strengthening of the PLC.

Action 1: Coalition building plays a central role in the success of a PLC. Obviously, a group of people who pool their resources and work together to advance their common interests will, generally speaking, meet with more success than those who do not. The best way to build a coalition is to show members how they will benefit by contributing positively to the greater good.

Action 2: Given the current state of the economy, most schools have no choice but to operate on tighter budgets, and they are doing it more than ever before. Shrinking financial resources mean that not everyone will receive what is asked for. Therefore, it is wise to let your colleagues know that you are doing all you can and keeping their priorities in mind. Reassuring them that you value their Standpoint is your safest bet to reducing competition over limited resources while promoting compromise.

Action 3: Sometimes members start to believe that tenure or experience entitles them to certain privileges. They need to be reminded that education is not about "us," but about what we can do for the students. Sure, there will be those who claim they could do more if only they received more. But it costs nothing to be a contributing member of the PLC working toward the common goal.

Action 4: If all of the above fail, then concentrate on making individual members accountable for their actions and mindful of their contributions to the greater good. Your colleagues may have gotten busy, forgotten, or lost interest altogether. It is up to you to remind them that they are part of the PLC, and that their professional obligation is to the school's Big Picture. They should not doubt the importance of their participation in the success of the school.

Collectively, we are stronger than me! Therefore, a strategy of *supporting the greater good rather than individual interests* helps keep this Standpoint alive in your PLC. Adopting a new perspective will lead to greater Solidarity among members and greater success for the PLC.

SOLIDARITY STRATEGY 4: REGULARLY ATTEND TO GROUP MAINTENANCE AND PROCESSES

This particular strategy is hard to practice faithfully. It can be a little awkward sitting down with others to discuss everyone's follow-through—or lack thereof—on any established school-wide team agreement or set of norms. If done regularly, though, the strategy may produce deep, lasting effects for the teams and the school as a whole. It would also help maintain natural conflict under control and, ultimately, encourage the growth and development of the group. Unfortunately, the number of schools that actually employ this strategy is not that high.

Earlier we cited Wiseman's (2008) and Morr's (2010) research. Their studies not only found that collaboration-rich PLCs show a tenacious focus on building effective teams, but have unearthed another significant piece of information. Their survey asked, among other questions, about the group's engagement in periodic "time-out" or "maintenance sessions" to address individual concerns about process or behaviors." Of 2,877 teachers who responded, this question showed the lowest calculated means.

It really didn't matter which way one sliced it—the study revealed similar results for every school. This implies that people do not typically evaluate the effectiveness of group processes and behaviors. When problems arise, issues are not dealt with openly, but instead are swept under the rug, setting the stage for even more tension inside the group. There the concerns are allowed to fester. In that event what would be the point of crafting agreements?

Austrian influential writer and management consultant Peter Drucker echoed this sentiment. "We now accept the fact that learning is a lifelong process of keeping abreast of change. And the most pressing task is to teach people how to learn," he declared. In other words, learning is a continual process, as are the behaviors necessary to keep a PLC alive and successful.

Everyone has had experience, at one point or another, with a person whose behaviors or actions ran opposite to the group's actual agreements. Whatever the motive, failing to address concerns may turn the actions into an unspoken norm for acceptable behavior. Needless to say, such a prospect would create a serious impediment to progress, more resentment, and bitterness. In this sense Struggle becomes the Achilles' heel of every group effort.

Four actions correspond to this strategy.

Action 1: When people come together to craft or revise their agreements, one agreement should refer to this strategy. For instance, the commitment might declare simply that the group will revisit agreements regularly to address individual and group concerns. Just be certain that the term *regularly* is clear to all. Plainly state the timeframe in terms of quarter, month, and so on. Also, whenever pressing issues or anxieties surface about certain behaviors or processes, the members must be flexible enough to come together as soon as possible to remedy the situation.

Action 2: Be they principals or teachers, the team leaders within a PLC must exemplify this strategy. Any concern about behavior and processes must be put in plain sight and handled by the members themselves. It is inadvisable to rake someone over the coals; doing so only adds fuel to the fire. Everyone has to be aware of the negative implications of poor communication, though this can make for a pretty tough conversation. Which perhaps explains why the data suggests few people do it.

Here are three great resources to assist in your dialogue on thorny topics:

- *Crucial Confrontations: Tools for Resolving Broken Promises, Violated Expectations, and Bad Behavior* by Patterson et al. (2004)—An easy, step-by-step method for holding others accountable without harming the relationship. Information about the authors' *Crucial Confrontations* two-day workshop and certification course can be found at www.vitalsmarts.com. The authors also published *Crucial Conversations*.
- *Nonviolent Communication: A Language of Life* by Rosenberg (2003)— The author offers stories, practical exercises, and role-plays that can better communication, strengthen relationships, build trust, and prevent conflict.
- *Verbal Judo: The Gentle Art of Persuasion* by Thompson and Jenkins (2004). The authors highlight the importance of listening and engaging people through empathy.

Action 3: When concerns arise about behavior, it is better to handle the situation individually rather than in a group setting. There is no point in admonishing a colleague in front of others. Doing so will only provoke verbal retaliation, thus escalating the dispute and creating a bad climate. However, school-wide and team agreements have to spell out when an issue should be handled individually and when the group should be permitted to intervene.

Action 4: When trust in a group is low and everyone is on pins and needles, it may be time for anonymity as you attend to group processes or behaviors. Perhaps the members could write their chief concerns on 3 x 5 index cards, which the group leader may read aloud. This would give everyone the opportunity to be heard, away from the tendency to use input from the most assertive voices. Over time trust must be recognized and developed, because too much of Action 4 and of anonymity can produce a group personality where members hide their Standpoint on a 3 x 5 index card. This balancing act takes time.

SOLIDARITY STRATEGY 5: USE A TEAM SURVEY INSTRUMENT TO DEVELOP TEAMWORK AND UNITY

Surveys are great tools for helping teams and organizations desiring continual improvement. Regular checkups will allow them to assess what is working and what is not, because surveys help members identify the discrepancies that separate the current condition from a desired state. Teams are the driving force of any PLC; therefore, no one can afford to wander aimlessly in search of the right intervention. Precise information will determine the diagnosis.

When it comes to teambuilding, there are many types of surveys. Some are long, others short, or are validated differently by the empirical data. The kind of survey we propose here is the forty-question instrument called the Four Key Foundations Assessment (figure 11.2). First introduced in Wiseman's (2010) *Strong Schools, Strong Leaders*, this survey assesses perceptions in each of the Four Key Foundations with a view to assisting employees in building effective teams.

The Four Key Foundations Assessment is a great help to teams that want to be cohesive, effective units working interdependently toward common school-wide goals. Richter (2012) observed that schools and teams that showed strong evidence of keeping to the Four Key Foundations also scored higher on tests. More specifically, he found a statistically significant difference on the Four Key Foundations between high-achieving schools and low-achieving schools. Based on his findings, he recommended that teams conduct assessments at least twice a year to serve as guideposts for success.

Here are some easy-to-follow actions to help schools and its members *use a team survey instrument to develop teamwork and unity.*

Action 1: Triangulate any existing qualitative and quantitative data to get a feel for the effectiveness of the teams throughout the campus. For

Strategies for Solidarity

Four Key Foundations Assessment

Directions: This instrument assesses your perceptions about the current reality of your school. Read each statement and then use the scale below to select the score that best reflects your personal degree of agreement with the statement. Be certain to select only one response for each statement. The first three sections (Listening to the People and the Environment, Building Agreements, and Co-Creating Purpose) focus on the school in general. The last section (Fostering Effective Teams) is aimed at determining information about the team(s) with which you belong.

Scale:
1 = Strongly Disagree   2 = Disagree   3 = Agree   4 = Strongly Agree

Foundation #1: Listening to People and the Environment	1	2	3	4
1. The leader frequently listens to staff members to seek ideas and input on key decisions.				
2. Meetings are regularly used to effectively make decisions and accomplish important tasks.				
3. The leader is able to sense when problems arise (both internal and external) and is proactive in addressing those problems.				
4. When staff members have a concern the leader listens and takes appropriate action in a timely manner.				
5. The leader participates democratically with staff members in the sharing of decision-making authority.				
6. When important decisions are made the leader consistently communicates the reasoning behind those decisions.				
7. Decisions are regularly made based on current data and information.				
8. The staff has frequent opportunities to formally and informally share ideas and suggestions for improvement.				
9. Everyone supports decisions even though they may not agree with them.				
10. Everyone assumes shared responsibility and accountability in important decisions without evidence of imposed power and authority.				

Foundation #2: Building Agreements	1	2	3	4
11. The staff's actions and behaviors are built on trust, respect and caring relationships.				
12. The staff perceives conflict and tension as an opportunity for growth.				
13. Differences of opinion between staff members exist and are discussed openly.				
14. Staff is comfortable communicating feelings and frustrations.				
15. When conflict or tension arises, each staff member addresses it in a constructive manner.				
16. The staff has formally established productive norms and commitments that define the way everyone should behave.				
17. The staff knows of and accepts the agreed upon behaviors and commitments.				
18. The staff consistently confronts those who are not following through with agreed upon behaviors and commitments.				
19. When changes occur (e.g., new members arrive, restructuring, initiatives, etc.) the staff regularly revisits the agreed upon behaviors and makes changes when necessary.				
20. The leader's actions always exemplify agreed upon behaviors and commitments.				

Foundation #3: Co-Creating Purpose	1	2	3	4
21. The staff functions with a strong sense of commitment and shared purpose.				
22. There exists a realistic and compelling vision and mission with recognizable goals that serve as guideposts.				
23. The accomplishment of short-term goals is celebrated often.				
24. The staff's actions are aligned with the vision, mission and goals.				
25. Each staff member's personal values, goals and aspirations are known and recognized.				
26. Each staff member's personal values, goals and aspirations are somehow interconnected with the overarching collective purpose.				
27. A collaborative process exists for developing shared purpose and commitment among the staff.				
28. The staff places the collective purpose on par with their personal ambitions.				
29. The leader regularly articulates and communicates the vision, mission and goals.				
30. Teams are focused and work interdependently to achieve the joint vision, mission and recognizable goals.				

Figure 11.2. Four Key Foundations Assessment

instance, find out the state of interpersonal relationships among the team members. Is conflict always getting in the way of progress? Do all the members support teams' decisions?

Action 2: Use the Four Key Foundations Assessment school-wide to validate existing data and to determine a baseline mean score for each

Foundation #4: Fostering Effective Teams	1	2	3	4
31. Team members share a common identity and work from a common set of beliefs.				
32. Team members work together (as opposed to working in isolation) in order to accomplish tasks.				
33. Feelings of trust exist within the team and among its members.				
34. The team's work environment is joyful or positive.				
35. Conflict among team members is openly dealt with; it is not allowed to fester.				
36. Team discourse surrounds high levels of listening and question asking.				
37. Risk-taking is encouraged while errors are tolerated and seen as opportunities for growth.				
38. Team members understand and accept the group's organizational structure and operational format.				
39. The group engages in periodic "time out" or "maintenance sessions" to address individual concerns about processes or behaviors.				
40. The team is aware of external factors and is pragmatic in its approach.				

Figure 11.3. Four Key Foundations Assessment Continued

question, as well as for each of the four foundations. Items with a preponderant response of "disagree" indicate areas in need of attention.

Action 3: Work collaboratively with staff to come up with "positive" interventions (or actions) that address the areas of weakness. Put your actions on paper, be transparent with intended plans, and implement.

Action 4: After employing "positive" interventions for some time, reassess using the Four Key Foundations Assessment, and repeat.

In chapters 14 and 15, we briefly discuss the power of action research in the effort to increase the overall effectiveness of teams and schools. Surveys may be a great aid to action research and organizational development, but we offer an additional tool—the 4S Learning Community Assessment (4S-LCA). Our tool assesses the evidence of each strategy presented in this book. Used in combination, these two instruments offer staff the necessary information to take their PLC from theory to practice.

SOLIDARITY STRATEGY 6: INCORPORATE INDIVIDUAL GOALS AND PASSIONS INTO THE ORGANIZATIONAL MISSION AND VISION

This strategy applies a commonly used business concept: *Get the right people in the right seats on the bus.* PLCs should take their cue from this. Finding a good fit is critical to achieving maximum efficiency, effectiveness, and fulfillment. Before that happens personal biases and differences must be put aside for the greater good of the school. Putting staff in positions and assignments where they can contribute their strengths and passions magnifies the potential of the PLC. The trick is to match personal passion with assignment.

The formerpresident of Fiji, Josefa Iloilo, once stated: "I will, from this day, strive to forge togetherness out of our differences." Obviously, he put the task of putting political differences aside for the greater good of his country. The same mind-set has to take hold in the PLC, while striving for Solidarity through Standpoint and Struggle.

Below are two actions for this strategy.

Action 1: Interview staff members and ask them about their personal passions, hobbies, and strengths. Too often we look for complicated solutions when the answer is really quite simple. The answer usually lies with the members. Therefore, schedule meetings with staff on their prep; then ask them what motivates, inspires, or drives them. People generally love to talk about their jobs and their lives. At worst, the interview process will reinforce personal relationships with staff.

Here is an example of personal connections in a PLC. A continuation high school needed more elective courses to improve high school graduation rates. Staff members were consulted until an English teacher was discovered to have a passion for creating websites and maintaining her personal website. This provided the perfect opportunity to add an elective course, where that teacher could pursue her passion and, at the same time, feel passionate about teaching. This perfect match brought the Beginning Webpage Design course into being.

Action 2: Give people assignments that tap into and match their passions as soon as you discover their true motivation. If no position matches the passion of a member, then challenge staff by asking: How can we find a course that both meets our need and taps into our collective talent?

A common theme—and obsession—among PLCs is student outcomes. Most of us enter the teaching profession to motivate students to learn and to enhance their lives. PLCs have to provide the conditions that allow them to use the personal passions of teachers in a way that leaves a positive impact on the students. Find those teachers and match each to an assignment that best taps into their passions.

SOLIDARITY STRATEGY 7: CELEBRATE PERSONAL AND PROFESSIONAL SUCCESSES

For PLCs to fulfill their potential they must function as an effective team. Celebrating personal and professional successes can amount to a powerful strategy for building Solidarity. Arroyo (2011) noted how successful PLCs used a strategy of balancing celebration against work to promote supportive relationships.

Tom Peters, an American writer on business management practices, recommends: "Celebrate what you want to see more of."

Such a simple sentence for a profound idea. Granted that getting the team members to know one another is a key characteristic of team effectiveness; but the heart and soul of this strategy is, first, understanding who your colleagues are as people and what they value. Understanding precedes the celebrating, bringing of staff together, and strengthening of the relationships on which the PLC is built. Understanding alone is cause for celebration.

Below are two actions for this strategy.

Action 1: Watch for personal and professional accomplishments to celebrate. Using e-mails, birthdays, and thank-you cards for that purpose is great. After all, children are born; they graduate and find personal achievement. This is the stuff of life, not just outside the school parameters but also inside. So take the time to let staff know that their lives are important.

Action 2: Set up a "secret spy network." This is a funny way to describe an anonymous system where members can drop the name and accomplishment of a colleague. It works well with many of the chores that staff quietly perform every day. The idea is to recognize the small things that make a big difference for both the members and the students.

SOLIDARITY STRATEGY 8: ENJOY FOOD AND PLAY TOGETHER

If Solidarity is the goal, then sharing joy is the right strategy to employ. Approach work with a genuine sense of joy. What better way to share joy and express feelings of good will than to break bread together? It happens everywhere. Men try to woo women by asking them out to dinner, because the act of sharing food is itself a message—a powerful one. Arroyo (2011) found that the presence of food during the staff meetings tended to strengthen relationships.

In the words of American basketball star and businessman Michael Jordan, "Just play. Have fun. Enjoy the game." Why? Because personal passion classed solely as "work" can trigger negative reactions in people. On the other hand, people sharing in their joys and happiness seem to rekindle the fire, and the classroom becomes a joy again.

Action 1: During staff, team, or department meetings, make sure there is food around. Even a small snack and mineral water will be positively interpreted. Sharing a meal together brings people closer. It has been like this since the dawn of history. Cooking for others is a sacred act; parents cook for their children. But *cooking* for staff members—as opposed to buying cheap, prepackaged food at the local supermarket—can be just as meaningful. Cooking for staff provides a stronger bonding experience.

Action 2: Cook or bake your culinary specialty for staff with the knowledge that no time spent making food for colleagues is wasted. People are liable to overlook other activities but not cooking. If you find cooking a challenge, then barbecue or make sandwiches. Whatever you do, put a genuine effort into breaking bread with the staff.

Action 3: To build Solidarity, spend time laughing together. Sadly, in the thick of our teaching activities, we frequently forget to enjoy each other's company. But being together, away from work, can engender powerful bonding experiences. It is not always easy, thanks to the workload, but PLC members have to find time to get together away from school. So start taking colleagues out to lunch; meet at a restaurant after school or plan an activity. It almost doesn't matter what kind of activity; just make sure it takes place outside the school, beyond the reach of the classroom and all its challenges.

Solidarity and teamness are closely connected to student achievement and, therefore, to PLC success. For student learning to advance in life, PLCs have no choice but to offer the appropriate Structure (the subject of the next section) and Solidarity as foundational elements. Without them no PLC can realize its potential.

IV

Structure

> Professional learning communities do not have to be within the same building or district; with the power of technology PLCs can stretch from across the hall to across the world.
> —Jacob Dunn, educational consultant

Effective Structure—the last quadrant in the 4S Approach—is critical to the PLC. Yet the most sophisticated structure in the world will still spawn confusion, dysfunction, and failure without three elements:

1. Clear recognition of each staff member's Standpoint.
2. Acknowledgment of the natural Struggle that accompanies these different points of view.
3. Building of effective teams through Solidarity.

This book provides the practitioner with realistic, practical, and applicable strategies for reviving the PLC in the shortest amount of time. Every other quadrant—Standpoint, Struggle, and Solidarity—leads to this high point for the PLC. The research on group dynamics and leadership demonstrates that if the staff is ready neither to hear the message nor to acknowledge the power of the PLC, then Structure will not work.

The final step is to create a Structure that will promote and support the effectiveness of your school PLC. As before, the following chapters present, first, a way of looking at Structure, and second, practical strategies to improve the structures supporting your PLC.

110 *Structure*

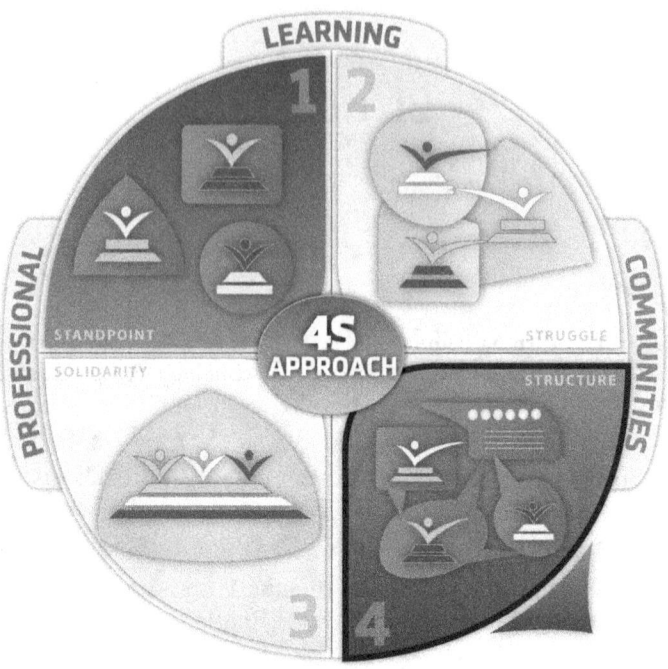

Figure 11.4.   The 4S Approach—Structure

TWELVE
The Chicken or the Egg?

> Professional Learning Communities are a microcosm of the world that must exist in education in order to allow teachers, counselors, and administrators to build a framework of opportunity and safety nets that meets the needs of the local community.
> —Dr. Joseph A. Guarino, director of curriculum, New Brighton, PA

WHAT IS STRUCTURE?

Past and current literature on PLCs has concentrated heavily on the impact of Structure upon student performance. In this book, Structure refers to the systems, arrangements, and organizations that should be in place. It implies the use of bell schedules, collaboration time, conference periods, positive reward systems, intervention programs, and other self-created systems for improving learning.

While necessary, moreover, Structure is only one of four components (quadrants). The first three quadrants—Standpoint, Struggle, and Solidarity—are basically *Relationships*. If the Relationship is meager, then system efficiency will break down. But it's a bit like the chicken-and-egg argument: Do positive Relationships come from effective Structure, or the other way around?

STRUCTURE WITH MEAGER RELATIONSHIPS

To explore the idea of a Structure without reference to productive Relationships let us take the example of house construction.

An expensive, extremely talented architect is hired to design and oversee a project. He or she draws up the design plan with intricate detail. It is well-thought out, user friendly, and, on paper, looks every bit the perfect home. Guess what came next? Construction, of course. Then, the architect needed a reality check.

It was easy enough to think up the plan, but so much money, time, and energy had apparently been spent on the design that the funding to hire skilled workmen to do the actual work had all but dried up. Instead of higher-end skills, therefore, the institution had settled for less skilled subcontractors. The result was poor workmanship, lack of communication, isolation, and inefficient work practices—the foundations were flawed, the walls imperfect, and the roofing inadequate. None of these defects were easy to fix.

One day, the homeowner came by to inspect the new home, visibly excited about the design and the possibilities it offered. He opens the front door ajar and then, lo and behold, reality sinks in. To his horror the foundation was cracked, imperfections pocked the walls, and water leaked through the roof. Can you picture the owner's reaction? She must have been as deeply disappointed as she was confused. The house looked great on paper but the execution was another story altogether.

Schools function in the same fashion. However elaborate their Structure design, it is the people inside the organization's systems who make the difference, thanks to their knowledge, skills, and ability to work together in groups and teams. It stands to reason, therefore, that they have to put their energies into forging Relationships that give them the power to implement decisions regarding the system.

Here is another example that shows how a Structure existing in a vacuum, without any Relationships, succumbs to an exercise in "spinning the wheels." An amazing architect comes along with the perfect design for a house, but the subcontractors are infighting and too busy making short shrift of the quality of the work, existing relationships, and important deadlines. Despite several visits by building inspectors, the work has not stayed up to code. Frustrated with the slow pace of the work and all the infighting, the architect decides to redesign the building using a whole new set of blueprints. Her hope is to remove at least some of the issues that have thwarted cooperation.

Imagine what the subcontractors are feeling. Weeks of work thrown out the window, right? What is this architect doing to us? They dig in their heels, insisting on a permanent set of blueprints before resuming their work. Tensions fester, and even less work gets done. In her attempt to resolve the situation, the architect accomplished the opposite effect than the one intended.

There is nothing wrong with either her intention or her promise of a new and better system. The staff's inability to work as a single team has undermined the previous system, no matter how perfect or imperfect it happened to be. Perfect designs with imperfect implementation cannot work.

RELATIONSHIPS WITH POOR STRUCTURE

Now, suppose that synergistic Relationships are active but lack adequate Structure. Will a better Structure evolve, or is that possibility doomed from the start?

Consider the problem in terms of the house construction analogy again. A carpenter, a plumber, and an electrician are hired for their professionalism and ability to work with others. In fact, their individual and collective skills have earned them a good deal of fame. They arrive at the job site early, each aware of the importance of getting to know the other subcontractor in the project. They get along famously and, after some shoptalk, acquire a better sense of how each goes about his work—in other words, they have become familiar with each other's Standpoints.

This positive feeling leads them to believe that Solidarity is emerging even before the work has begun. Another hour passes and the architect still has not shown up. The three men bear no ill will toward one another, but they get a little antsy about maintaining their high standards of work. So they decide to start building the house without the blueprints. After all, they had worked on countless sites before and knew their respective trades inside out.

Lacking a "system," though, they quickly run into difficulties. Despite their best collective intentions, each craftsman puts his own perspective forward, based on his respective area of expertise. The result? A fragmented conception of what the house ought to look like. To their credit, though, they stick with it.

When they were done the house boasted the most amazing system of plumbing; the framing was strong; and the electrical fixtures were second to none. The only problem was it all looked like a toddler's painting—without a doubt the worst-looking structure on the block. As ugly as it appeared, though, it had beautiful fixtures and, most importantly, sturdy frames and a rock-solid foundation to withstand the elements of nature. If the walls are perfect, the roof is airtight, and the foundation is as smooth as a baby's bottom, then something must have come out right. This minimal outcome fulfills the main purpose of any construction. Better yet, all the homeowners have to do next is to undertake a few interior and exterior modifications to alter the uncomely looks of the house.

A real school setting would have drawn attention to some lacuna in how the project was being handled. The school may not have any formal Structure in place to address the situation, but by bringing the PLC members together and attending to the Relationships, something might still come to life. Capacity comes from collective wisdom.

Attending to Relationships first allows effective Structure to evolve from the creativity and innovation of the members themselves. The ideal scenario is when the members realize enough of their potential to permit them to innovate and create Structure for higher levels of success.

This is exactly why the first three sections of our book treat of ideas on building relationships and teamwork. But if the hierarchical structure in place includes a cracked slab, weak frame, or permeable roof, then flattening it may be in order.

What comes first in a PLC, Relationships or Structure?

Here is a more direct way to pose the question: Would you rather work in a school with a shaky foundation, weak frame, and a leaky roof because you happen to like its glitter? Or would you prefer a school standing on a sound Structure even though it looks—to put it mildly—"unorthodox"?

PLC Structure depends on the will to create Relationships, because Relationships—whether supportive or dysfunctional—give free rein to culture, climate, and expectations. In short, there is no sound Structure without will.

THE FUNDAMENTAL STRUCTURE

Genuine PLC success implies a Structure built with healthy Relationships. In response to the chicken-and-egg paradox above—whether Relationships foster successful Structure or vice versa—the interdependence between these two components begins in earnest only with a strong commitment to Relationships.

Healthy Relationships comprise the high-powered engine that drive the PLC; the fundamental Structure helps the members carry out their interactions in a more systematic, deliberate fashion. The capacity to prepare the conditions (time, venue, and opportunity) for collaboration is a valuable resource—on par with money, data bank, and facilities, because collaborative work has to be made part of the schedule. Failing that, Relationships will not play their proper constructive role.

Dedicated staff and teachers go beyond the call of duty to spend countless hours trying to improve things in their schools. If they are dedicated enough, they will not act in isolation and, at the same time, expect lasting results. Their bottom line is that a PLC needs a school-wide culture that ensures learning for all students, or it is nothing. Accordingly, their school schedules must allocate the time staff and teachers alike need to work together.

The path to a successful PLC is not linear but more like a winding road filled with potholes and obstacles. Structure and member dedication will provide the necessary strategy.

THIRTEEN
Levels of Professional Learning Community Effectiveness

> [A PLC] is connecting with people for students. It is an essence that a visitor feels when they walk into the school.
> —Dale S. Rumberger, site administrator

The 4S Approach stands on long reflections by the authors regarding the impact of each quadrant on the development of the PLC. Clearly, quadrants promote member collaboration via Standpoint, Struggle, and Solidarity, and each addresses some aspect of group dynamics that, if overlooked, may threaten rather than promote the development of the PLC.

Structure, the last Quadrant, establishes the rules by which the members and PLC must abide and act. In addition to being the easiest candidate for improvement, Structure can also provide proof to outsiders that serious steps have been taken to improve student performance. In fact, a letter touting the benefits of the new bell schedule would offer parents a good glimpse at ongoing efforts.

However, Structure can too quickly become the sole focus. While important for assigning meeting opportunities and outlining the processes to be followed, it is nevertheless less vital to the overall development and growth of the PLC than the other three quadrants. Let us expand on the subject with reference to the four Levels of PLC Effectiveness.

LEVELS OF PLC EFFECTIVENESS

Like a living organism, the PLC is constantly changing—in flux. It gains experience with each new addition, loss, interaction, success, or failure of its members. How the PLC deliberately and collaboratively uses this experience makes all the difference. Its efforts will either decrease or increase value, depending on how well it can integrate member Standpoint, Struggle, and Solidarity. Three quadrants help develop the Relationships needed to carry out the functions of a successful PLC. Structure, on the other hand, operates more to establish formally recognized rules, policies, and procedures.

Let's take a closer look at each of the four Levels of PLC Effectiveness depicted in figure 13.1.

LEVEL 1: INCAPACITATED PLC

This is the lowest Level of PLC Effectiveness. A PLC at this level is characterized by ineffective Structure and Meager Relationships and, therefore, an inability to perform normally. Needless to say, this makes for a dysfunctional school culture and does not necessarily suggest the early beginnings of a community. Moreover, lacking a formal Structure and member Relationships, an Incapacitated PLC can lumber on for years.

Incapacitated PLC is not a level at which you want your school to find itself. Here, the school's organizational Structure offers little support for future progress; common procedures such as monitoring attendance and dividing hallway duties are all absent; communication among faculty, staff, and administration is infrequent and ineffective.

In some cases, member communication may take on conflict and competition over the school's limited resources. Meeting times, if any, turn into complaint sessions. However, with few Structures in place—for ex-

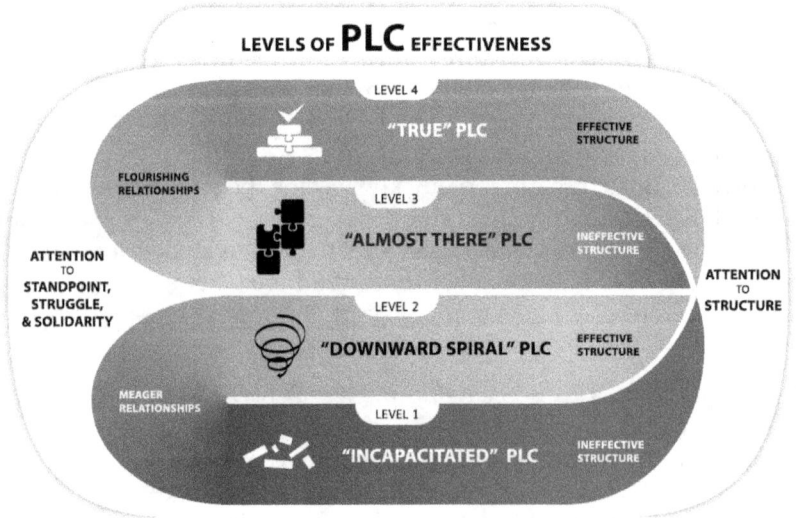

Figure 13.1. Levels of PLC Effectiveness

ample, grade- or department-level teams—members still have to discuss pressing issues like student discipline, parent/teacher conferences, and upcoming special events. Only, the expectations and opportunities for shared member leadership are nearly nonexistent. The principal, having developed the school's vision and mission on his own, will side with the faction that can best sell his agenda to the rest of the staff.

In short, ineffective Structure and Meager Relationships will leave your school operating from day to day with only intermittent planning; it risks keeping what scarce resources are at your disposal disorganized or misused. Administrative shortcomings will be rife. Lacking all the necessary components of a true PLC, the Incapacitated PLC deprives itself of the combined strength of its members and, instead, becomes a babysitting service, far away from the values of learning and achievement it claims to espouse.

LEVEL 2: DOWNWARD SPIRAL PLC

A PLC at this level is characterized by effective Structure but Meager Relationships. It cannot help going around in circles as it sinks ever-deeper into dysfunction. A Downward Spiral PLC may have the formal Structure to succeed, but it has to improve the quality of collaboration among its members in order to achieve healthier Relationships.

Here is what happens in a struggling school seeking to rearrange its bell schedule, meeting times and places, and teachers' rooms and assignments. Though convinced that this is the path to raising student performance, their efforts at implementation will stop there, because implementing formal Structure is a reactive, even reciprocal process. While some teachers will no doubt welcome the latest changes, others will sigh for the old beaten path of doing things. Others still will question the usefulness of changes on top of previous initiatives.

Without their constructive feedback, there is little chance anyone will come out of this process pleased. When push comes to shove, the teachers will no doubt acquiesce to the changes. After all, they have been meeting whenever they were told to meet, teaching where and what they were told to teach. Too used to going through the motions, they will neither understand nor entertain any special desire to promote the next set of changes.

True, things can still "get done" at their meetings, in spite of the competition and conflict among the members. Besides a collaborative environment, though, they lack the will to invest value in a common school-wide culture. An organization like that cannot well call itself a Community, much less a PLC. Although a Downward Spiral PLC will still tell the members when and where to meet, it has few means to instruct them on how to act and interact during meetings. This failure of relationships can clog up an entire organization.

Rearranging the bell schedule, meeting times and places, and teachers' rooms and assignments may be formalities, but they can be turned into vehicles for the development of member Relationships and cultural unity, which happen to be the real drivers.

LEVEL 3: "ALMOST THERE" PLC

This, the third level of PLC Effectiveness, displays an ineffective Structure but Flourishing Relationships. An Almost There PLC is nearly a true PLC. Ineffective Structure hampers its success, even if the members show a healthy willingness to work around the system on behalf of student achievement.

Unfortunately, there is no panacea to every malaise, because no two PLCs are identical. Schools are composed of individuals and create their own unique culture. Student size and demographics alike draw the individuals who want to develop this culture. That is not to say that schools should not look to other schools for guidance. Still, each school must look within itself for the answers to its problems by developing its own unique culture and PLC. Formal Structure becomes effective only when the PLC has developed Solidarity, which in turn results from the Struggle to incorporate all member Standpoints.

From this perspective, Flourishing Relationships will help overcome ineffective Structure and strengthen the PLC as a whole. Just as no two experiences are similar, however, no two PLCs can be the same. The difference is that PLCs with a well-developed, inclusive culture are not limited by either formal or ineffective Structure for their internal communication and collaboration. Their trusting community has the capacity to share teaching practices and ideas for growth, not to speak of common values. An inclusive culture on this pattern allows all those who participate in it the opportunities to contribute. No single select group of faculty suffices in driving the school forward any longer. This community has chosen a process that seeks to include all the members, thereby decreasing the risk of burnout among educators too burdened and stretched thin by their commitments and responsibilities.

Under these propitious conditions, the members have the chance for once to be proactive, rather than reactive in the manner of the second level. They have the power to take the reins and to develop their own unique culture regardless of the formal Structure.

LEVEL 4: TRUE PROFESSIONAL LEARNING COMMUNITY

Characterized by effective Structure and Flourishing Relationships, this is the highest Level of PLC Effectiveness. It embodies the very concept of PLC, where members work together within a supportive Structure to raise student performance. A True PLC that has successfully reinvented itself wields the power to recognize, plan, and implement any changes necessary for fulfilling the goals, mission, and vision of the school.

A True PLC will take shape if the school has grown dissatisfied with its conditions. It pursues its vision for the future by identifying a course of action without which member Relationships have no prospect of improving. Having reached such a high level, a PLC clearly has discovered inclusion amid member diversity; it has overcome wasteful competition and conflict, reinventing the group into a cohesive team.

Thanks to the thoughtful, calculated effort of its members, there is now a PLC. But this hardly means that the PLC requires no further support or guidance from all members. On the contrary, a True PLC plans and implements the changes necessary to realizing its objectives further afield. Besides that, it has to determine and overcome the root causes of unproductive or ineffective Structure and any negative behaviors and attitudes. The Structure it has built should receive the support of all the members by developing a sense of buy-in and belonging. By recognizing and valuing all of its stakeholders, it can forge strong support networks, where all members may contribute their strengths and commitment to fulfilling the Community vision.

All in all, moving to higher levels requires teachers and principals to spend the time up front attending to Relationships!

FOURTEEN
Strategies for Structure

> Our professional development is job embedded and on going, born from need and suggested by the study of our data, primarily from the teachers themselves. They're becoming experts in various facets of the curriculum and we share our expertise. They know results matter.
> —Lynne Griffiths, principal, Redwood City, CA

So far we have examined twenty-four proven strategies for staff to handle Standpoint, Struggle, and Solidarity. This chapter will describe the most successful strategies for Structure: eight practices that PLCs can undertake to cultivate collaboration and increased achievement. While it is important to develop the Relationship quadrants (Standpoint, Struggle, and Solidarity), one must establish effective formal Structure that members not only may operate, but also stand a good chance of excelling in.

The following strategies will provide your school with the best opportunity to become a True PLC.

1. Provide time, location, and opportunity for collaboration.
2. Give teachers and teams the autonomy to deliver instruction, intervention, and enrichment.
3. Take an action research approach.
4. Create a system for site-based professional development.
5. Employ systematic, tiered intervention systems.
6. Integrate a laser-focused common assessment system for academic monitoring.
7. Implement school-wide acknowledgment systems for students.
8. Employ a learning community survey to drive school-wide practices.

Chapter 14

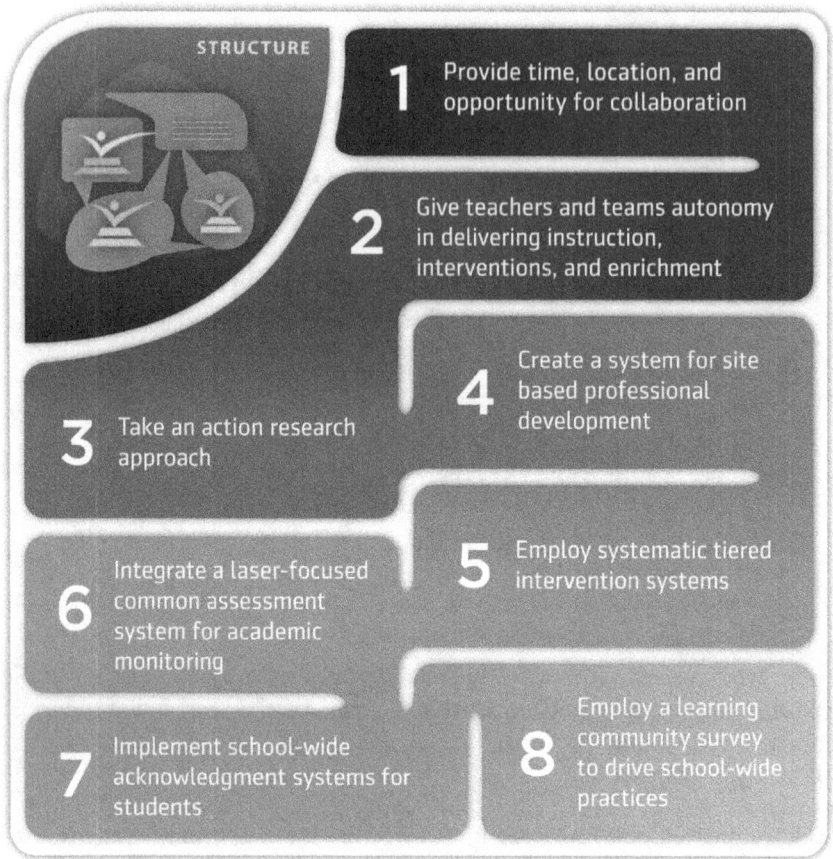

Figure 14.1. Eight Strategies for Structure

STRUCTURE STRATEGY 1: PROVIDE TIME, LOCATION, AND OPPORTUNITY FOR COLLABORATION

It has become commonplace for people to identify the time or location of a meeting with the spirit of the PLC. Time, venue, opportunities are essential to the PLC. The question is how to get staff members to learn from one another in a deliberate effort to improve practices. This is practically impossible in the absence of a collaborative spirit.

Working inside the four walls of a classroom—day in, day out—will not cut it. Physical presence is not enough. Where are the regular and focused interactions? This is where time, location, and opportunities come in. Without them group members will stick to their respective myopic worlds; practices will stagnate because there is no alternative. Isolation is the norm.

District and site leaders with the wisdom to support the PLC can create a Structure that allows staff to come together often for important work, using interdisciplinary teams, departments, and committees.

Action 1: Allocate regular time for collaboration within the contracted workday. *Strengthening union and administration relationships*—the Standpoint strategy introduced in chapter 5—is a precursor to this action. Union and management leaders at the district level have to be able to work in partnership, allocating regular time for collaboration, whether for the purpose of redesigning the school-year calendar or proposing a memorandum of understanding.

The traditional "hour-long, once or twice a month" staff meeting leaves little time for serious work. Meetings tend to take the press-briefing approach because general information, among other things, has to be disseminated.

Labor and management teams in many districts use the recommended strategy of allotting regular, distraction-free time for professional development, some employing a modified day once a week. Students, on those days, start school a half-hour or so later than usual in the morning to permit staff to meet. Another option is for the students to be released early so the school staff could meet in the afternoon. Other districts assign a certain number of days per month for professional development.

There are many ways in which schools can rearrange their time, assuming the aim is to work as a community of learners. Though districts have to make it a priority, this action is much easier said than done, requiring lots of feedback. In this venture, obviously, the entire community—especially the students' families—has to be aware and supportive of any changes in students' start times, end times, and days off. The new arrangement of the school day must also meet any requirements pertaining to instructional minutes. Lastly are the elaborate bussing schedules, which may have to be overhauled to accommodate the change.

Action 2: Create a master schedule as a means to instill a "teaming" approach that allows for time and the opportunities for authentic collaboration. But there are so many other things to consider—the number of students at each grade level, required courses and electives, students' proficiency levels, double blocks versus single blocks, English learners, the number of periods in a day, students with disabilities, teachers' credentials and strengths, conference periods, and so on.

Rather than burden the reader with the nuts and bolts of master scheduling, which would require another book, let us call this action item a call for creative scheduling that aims to place teachers strategically in teams according to their strengths and personalities. Regular common planning time for interdisciplinary teams or departments banishes the self-contained insularity at the team level. There is not one right way to do it; every school's schedule is unique.

Action 3: Once or twice a month, allocate time to rotate half-day meetings. This is your last resort if actions 1 and 2 lie beyond reach despite the authentic face-to-face interactions between students and their teachers. This option has to be carried out even if the Structure of the district or school seems incapable of determining either the times or the opportunities for collaboration. Voluntary meetings may still take place after school and on weekends. However, because this type of meeting cannot be mandatory—nor, for that matter, can it represent all the different perspectives or Standpoints—it should be used to foster collaborative efforts.

Action 4: Use technology to enhance collaboration. For instance, teachers can avail themselves of online document files and server-based locations to share documents virtually. These tools can be made to work together to develop lesson plans, assessments, and other tasks. Another significant resource for enhancing collaboration is social media.

STRUCTURE STRATEGY 2: GIVE TEACHERS AND TEAMS AUTONOMY IN DELIVERING INSTRUCTION, INTERVENTIONS, AND ENRICHMENT

When it comes to instruction, intervention, and enrichment staff members may be well-informed but usually from their own niche. They are involved in Special Education programs and strategies; others are skilled at working with gifted students, at reading or in math; or perhaps they are unfamiliar with the concept of PLC but more adept at applying grade-level standards. All these skill sets—Standpoints, in a sense—will enrich the PLC.

Still, only a select few educators—whether principals or teachers—understand everything under the sun about classroom instruction. Who in his right mind thinks he could wrap his head around every standard, in every content area? Who has mastered a successful strategy and practice for every learner and learning style? More likely, the principal doesn't know it all, nor does the team leader, department chair, or anyone else for that matter.

Ulrich (1996) said, "Future leaders will have to master teamwork . . . and work with and through others because no one person can possibly master all the divergent sources of information necessary to make good decisions" (p. 213). This ought to be the mind-set of principals and teachers in a PLC. Principals are not the only people who create school-wide Structure, especially with regard to instruction, interventions, and enrichment. Teachers too should be informed of the parameters for content delivery, allocated time for teamwork, and entrusted with the task of bringing student learning to a new level.

Action 1: Develop and communicate school-wide goals based on current data. These goals help drive the planning for instruction, interventions, and enrichment, where different goals necessitate different Structures. As mentioned in our chapter on Strategies for Standpoint, a variety of processes and meeting designs can assist schools collectively to develop high, achievable targets.

Action 2: Create proper parameters for instruction, interventions, and enrichment within which teacher teams could work. Autonomy without limits leads to unnecessary work—and at worst, a free-flying circus. The three factors above may include the development and implementation of common assessments for monitoring learning, available resources to support additional duties or purchases, adherence to any laws and education codes set forth, and so forth.

Action 3: Create and implement delivery, intervention, and enrichment systems. Those entrusted with this considerable undertaking no doubt will take pride. The teachers' teams should take up the challenge of using their creativity to find genuine solutions, rather than just settle for a run-of-the-mill Structure, or business as usual. Artificial sticking points such as bells, schedules, and attendance scans should be kept at bay.

STRUCTURE STRATEGY 3: TAKE AN ACTION RESEARCH APPROACH

Whether the school is doing well or not, the staff will know. After all, the PLC is a living organism. Reflexively, staff would rather fail and know why than to succeed and completely miss the point.

Wiseman (2010) talks about the "Knowledge/Success Matrix" (figure 14.2), a mental process that associates *success* and *failure* with *knowing* and *not knowing*. Principals and teachers—operating at the level of the first quadrant—prefer to know the exact reason for their success. They can know by simply employing an action research approach while addressing everyday issues and solving problems.

Generally speaking, action research consists of diagnosing a Situation in Need of Attention (SITNA); it also gathers baseline data, employs a "positive" intervention (or action), and after some time, evaluates whether or not the intervention worked. If it did, the action may be resumed. If not, then one of two courses has to be pursued: either the intervention is tweaked or it is thrown out and it's back to the drawing board. The same cyclical longitudinal process is repeated again and again until the desired state is achieved.

Here are some simple, straightforward actions when applying the action research model.

Action 1: Frame the situation. Take some time out and make an effort to view your ongoing activities "from the balcony," so to speak. The balcony analogy comes from what Heifetz and Linsky (2002) described as "Getting off the Dance Floor and Going to the Balcony."

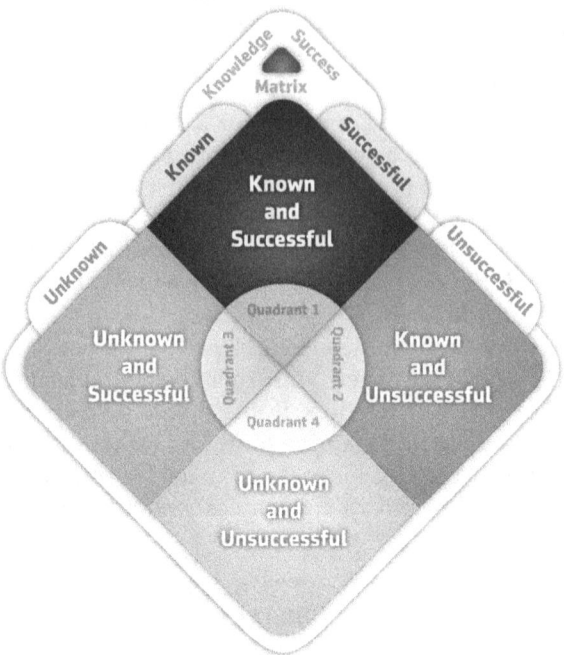

Figure 14.2. Knowledge/Success Matrix

> Few practical ideas are more obvious or more critical than the need to get perspective in the midst of action. Any military officer, for example, knows the importance of maintaining the capacity for reflection, even in the "fog of war." Great athletes can at once play the game and observe it as a whole—as Walt Whitman described it, "being both in and out of the game." Jesuits call it, "contemplation in action." Buddhists call it "karma yoga," or mindfulness. We call this skill "getting off the dance floor and going to the balcony," an image that captures the mental activity of stepping back in the midst of action and asking, "What's really going on here?" (p. 52)

Action 2: Assess the situation. It may be that teachers are using achievement or behavioral data to refine their practices systematically, or that team members have enlisted a team survey in their effort to develop group cohesiveness. If the aim is to improve the school as a whole, then this might involve interviews, focus groups, observations, or other data helpful in finding the best solution for the organization.

It may also involve a school-wide assessment tool like the 4S Learning Community Assessment (4S-LCA), which will be explained later. To avoid creating the impression of a smoke-and-mirrors process, it is important to disclose the available data to key stakeholders. Whatever the nature of the data, this scenario surely presents a learning opportunity.

Action 3: Diagnose the problem. The data tell a story, making any discrepancy between the current condition and a desired state (or SITNA) clearer. The members of the PLC should triangulate their sources of information, matching their diagnosis to a specific dysfunction.

Action 4: Plan and implement solutions. With the data out in the open and the SITNA well known, the PLC should bring everyone to the table for serious planning and action. At this point inclusive meeting designs come into play. The goal is to arrive at solutions that value everyone's unique Standpoint.

Principals and teachers have no time to waste spinning their wheels with programs, behaviors, or practices that demonstrate no impact on either student or adult learning. PLCs should have the ability to use the data in a methodical, scientific manner. The resulting change will happen in "Frame, Assess, Diagnose, and Plan" loops.

STRUCTURE STRATEGY 4: CREATE A SYSTEM FOR SITE-BASED PROFESSIONAL DEVELOPMENT

The fourth strategy for Structure pertains to professional development at the site level. Most districts can offer professional development opportunities opened up by any important issue. Every school, though, also possesses its unique collective Standpoint, strengths, needs, and combined expertise. The *answers lie inside the room.*

Its strategy aimed at *providing time, location, and opportunity for collaboration* in place, the PLC can now benefit from times and opportunities to work on a variety of activities that relate to the needs of the site throughout the year. This may take the form of teachers sharing strategies validated through action research, or developing intervention and enrichment activities for the students. More time should be allocated for later strategies—such as tiered interventions, common formative assessments, or school-wide acknowledgment systems.

Regardless of the issues or topics in the pipeline, or whether they originate in the state legislature or the district, every school staff has the potential to succeed via purposeful professional development. Whether it refines Structure or extends content knowledge and strategies, as a body the PLC has the capacity to overcome any obstacle.

Here are some actions to consider while making use of site-based professional development:

Action 1: Grant every member of the school the opportunity to be a part of a professional development team. The principal, or co-administrator, should not be the only decision maker with a focus on areas or activities in professional development. This has to be a school-wide initiative. Whenever only a select few are involved in the planning group, members tend to go through the motions. Involvement in the process, on the other hand, breeds commitment to learning.

Action 2: Use school-wide achievement and behavioral data to determine the direction of professional development for the whole year. Professional development is valuable when it can meet the needs of each member of the PLC. Therefore, create and share a tentative, flexible year-long calendar outlining objectives and activities. The professional development team should meet regularly, perhaps monthly, to revise the calendar and to address any issues that may arise. Staff may help with the planning by giving the team regular feedback on the usefulness of various professional development activities.

Action 3: Document the conversations in all professional development team meetings. One member of the professional development team should be responsible for both record keeping and the "end products." Copious notes highlighting both successes and struggles will better help the PLC plan professional development in the future.

STRUCTURE STRATEGY 5: EMPLOY SYSTEMATIC TIERED INTERVENTION SYSTEMS

Few educators have trouble relating to the concept of response to intervention (RTI) and the three-tiered pyramid. RTI is a key practice in PLCs where students receive increasingly intensive, research-based interventions based on their individual needs. It aims, first and foremost, to deliver high-quality, research-based instruction to all students and to intervene quickly with students struggling with academic, behavior, and attendance issues. Early identification and intervention are vital.

In the RTI model, tier I refers to the preventive school-wide Structure that students inherit. Pedagogically, this suggests a core instruction in the classroom, differentiation, flexible groupings, and so forth. Behaviorally, it entails universal expectations, explicit school-wide instruction in social skills, active supervision, acknowledgment systems, and so on. Traditionally, tier I has meant success for eighty to ninety percent of the student body.

Should students find no success in this tier, then tier II will offer supplementary—and systematic—interventions. Some common tier II interventions for academic and behavioral issues include support classes with smaller teacher-student ratios, behavioral or academic contracts, flexible scheduling and regrouping based on needs, and targeted skill development—to name but a few practices.

Finally, tier III aims to help the greatest number of students at risk of failure. Here, students with intensive needs receive specialized individualized services. Approximately three to five percent of students in a school fall in this category. Oftentimes, this includes students with disabilities, English language learners, and students targeted by the Child Find.

Thanks to the three tiers, students receive instruction at their instructional level and concepts are scaffolded up to grade-level standards. The result is that students suffer fewer transitions, gain more time, and enjoy numerous opportunities for response and interaction.

Based on this rudimentary outline of systematic tiered intervention systems, here are some critical actions that PLCs can undertake in the delivery of effective, high-quality services to all students.

Action 1: Assess and tweak existing programs and systems that support student learning. DuFour et al. (2006) posed the following critical questions, which help guide the ongoing "conversation":

- What knowledge and skills should the student acquire?
- How will we know when each student has acquired basic knowledge and skills?
- How will we respond to those students who have not learned?
- How will we respond to those students who have achieved the intended outcomes? (p. 21)

Schools that fail either to answer these questions precisely or to present a systematic response Structure have their work cut out for them. PLCs have to put in place the proper mechanisms and supports to ensure that all students can learn at the expected levels.

Action 2: Subject the student body to regular universal screening in order to identify potential struggling students. This step is critical to RTI, and is normally conducted school-wide three times a year (fall, winder, and spring). Not only is school-wide universal screening conducive to a proactive identification of at-risk students for the purpose of intervention, but the whole-school data can assist in evaluating the effectiveness of any school-wide initiative or practice that has been put in place.

Action 3: Frequently monitor the performance of the student's progress in each tier. Those that receive support in the second and third tiers should be monitored more regularly, perhaps every other week. Is every student responding to the intervention? Is he or she demonstrating growth? Most likely, some students do, while others are flat-lining. And when students remain stagnant, it's time to stop wasting everyone's time and employ different interventions or strategies.

PLCs have to continue their interventions with students demonstrating success, but they must also be able to quickly modify the interventions and practices with unsuccessful students. Persisting in an intervention that has not worked with certain students is a waste of time.

Tier I monitoring need not be as frequently applied as the other tiers. Moreover, a multitude of indicators may be used at this level—for instance, by *integrating a laser-focused common assessment system for academic monitoring,* the next strategy. District benchmarks can be useful in this regard.

Students identified as needing tier II supports are not necessarily "intervention lifers" if the Structure can promptly address their individual needs and seamlessly move them in and out of interventions in the course of the year. The important thing is for tiered interventions to be firmly rooted in uninterrupted, data-based decision making.

STRUCTURE STRATEGY 6: INTEGRATE A LASER-FOCUSED COMMON ASSESSMENT SYSTEM FOR ACADEMIC MONITORING

Schools with PLC systems in place, and that encourage collaboration among teachers and teams through frequent monitoring of student growth, study student progress regularly in all content areas. Instruction is repeatedly adapted to individual, classroom, and departmental needs.

The Structure that best enables staff to monitor student learning consists of a system of laser-focused common assessments. Here the individual teachers, teams, departments, and the school as a whole keep watch over all the students and their subgroups, regularly assessing them and tailoring instruction to meet their needs. This model has two main objectives. First, to provide a means to monitor the progress of all the students, informing staff as to which students require remediation and which enrichment. And second, to provide a vehicle for teacher collaboration and the sharing of best practices.

Individual and collective assessments are the driving force behind the ongoing conversations for performance improvement. But they have to match expected outcomes and improve instruction dramatically. Trying to achieve a match is not, however, a fly-by-night practice. It involves deep commitment, buy-in, and a devotion to data-driven decision making by every staff member.

Here are a handful of actions for getting a focused common assessment system off the ground.

Action 1: Involve everyone in the implementation and coordination, which should be well organized and structured. It is important to *go slow to go fast*. So the first action should aim to bring the staff together and begin the planning, little by little. This may take place over a series of meetings, preferably at the beginning of the school year—though midyear should not be considered a serious hindrance.

During their initial meetings teachers must be given adequate time and explicit direction for unpacking and deconstructing state standards, determining essential standards, getting a feel for the types of questions asked on accountability measures, and organizing those essential standards into site-based pacing schedules. If the district already has general pacing guides, any site-developed guidelines will support the direction of the district.

Action 2: Design a master calendar for common assessment by noting the dates by which teams of teachers should complete each assessment, but also include a range of dates for administering each assessment. Explicit timelines will help keep track of all assessments conducted during the year.

It is highly recommended that common, formative assessments be administered no less than once a month for each content area. Mathematics, science, and physical education assessments, for example, may be administered school-wide every other week; and language arts, social studies, and elective assessments perhaps once every three weeks. Another option is to allow all content area assessment administrations to coincide. Each department has to find the course of action that best fits the situation.

Action 3: Teachers regularly meet to develop tightly aligned common, formative assessments. No assessment should exceed twenty to twenty-five problems. It also has to balance different levels of thinking. Completion may take the students a full period to complete.

Here are some sources that discuss, in detail, assessments in the classroom:

- *Common Formative Assessments: A Toolkit for Professional Learning Communities* by Bailey and Jakicic (2012).
- *Common Formative Assessments: How to Connect Standards-Based Instruction and Assessment* by Ainsworth and Viegut (2006).
- *Classroom Assessment and Grading That Work* by Marzano (2006).

Action 4: Develop a mechanism to hold each teacher and team accountable for the implementation. A way to do this is for each team to design its own assessment, which it then submits to the principal or some other designee for content evaluation and to monitor team fidelity to established timelines.

This step must not be skipped, otherwise the Structure will lose momentum. Nowadays many schools and districts have access to online assessment management systems that input teacher-generated tests and complementary answer keys. Basically, someone inputs each assessment and answer key into the online database; student answer documents may then be printed out, along with the class sets of the test for subsequent student use.

Once each assessment has been administered, someone scans the student's answer sheet, producing immediate results online. Teachers who adhere to this system need not worry about the logistics of getting the student scans printed or graded, leaving them free to concentrate on their lesson plans, activities, and the next common assessment.

Action 5: Analyze the data and discuss struggling students. Regular analysis of the data helps narrow the achievement gap. Teams typically agree to split up their classrooms. One teacher takes those students who need to be retaught concepts, while another offers students who have mastered the standards more challenging lessons. However, the students themselves should have ample opportunity to demonstrate mastery of each concept. For example, if a student initially fails an assessment, he or she is accorded a second chance in the form of a retake, following additional small group instruction and reteaching of lessons.

When the teams of teachers come together to analyze the data, the students (and their groups) who have not met grade-level standards on the common assessments may be referred to after-school, before-school, or weekend programs. Individual teachers should be able to discern quickly their students' strengths and weaknesses in order to accelerate the intervention.

Teachers will become practiced at funneling students into the appropriate intervention and enrichment programs, relaying what particular topics or areas of deficit need to be addressed. Consequently, their students will receive targeted instruction and interventions designed to meet their needs.

This Structure, based as it is on a focused common assessment system, should be allowed to evolve over time. Implementation in the first year will likely prove difficult. The exams may not yet be drawn up, even though the teachers are on strict deadlines to collaborate. In subsequent years, though, the process will become refined as the teachers use the same exams, which they can modify as needed (changing, adding, or omitting questions).

Schmoker (2004) affirmed the importance of this Structure. "It starts," he wrote, "when a group of teachers meet regularly as a team to identify essential and valued student learning, develop common formative assessments, analyze current levels of achievement, set achievement goals, and then share and create lessons and strategies to improve upon those levels" (p. 48).

STRUCTURE STRATEGY 7: IMPLEMENT SCHOOL-WIDE ACKNOWLEDGMENT SYSTEMS FOR STUDENTS

In a PLC, struggling and high-achieving students alike are entitled to have their achievements celebrated. The problem is that schools merely give formal recognition to their efforts, usually the higher-achieving ones. It may take place every few months at some *rah-rah!* awards assembly. But what about the hundreds of other students in the crowd? How often are they acknowledged for their hard work?

Implementing school-wide acknowledgment systems for students is a process that recognizes individual students every day of the year. More broadly, it is about creating a school culture with the capacity to celebrate *the way we do things around here*. Celebrations have to reach everyone, inclusively, if they are to be celebrations of anything. What does the socioeconomic level of the school's clientele matter if the academic performance, attendance, behavior, and involvement in extracurricular activities of every student have to be recognized?

Although a school-wide acknowledgment system is just a slice of the Positive Behavioral Interventions and Supports (PBIS) initiative, the endproduct is what counts. The PLC Structure presented below, successfully implemented by a school, is one of the best we have seen. Think of a school located in one of the most impoverished, gang-infested neighborhoods around. Families have struggled for generations and the parents themselves had trouble finishing their schooling as kids. This inspired the staff to come together and develop a structured program where students could feel successful for their achievements, no matter how big or small those achievements may be.

The process they had in mind was comprehensive enough to involve many people. Both certificated and classified staff wanted to develop something that promised to increase student achievement, improve attendance, decrease suspensions and expulsions, and equally importantly, involve more students in extracurricular activities.

An avalanche of ideas later, the staff came up with a creative student incentive program that ended up transforming the culture of the school from top to bottom.

Now that a successful Structure has been implemented, the students can wake up every morning excited to put their better foot forward, because their attitude—with the parents and staff—is that *this is the way we do things around here*. Clearly, something good has taken root at that school. This "way of doing things" clearly provides the students with the opportunity to earn merits (or points) every day of the year for excellence in academics, behavior, attendance, and involvement in extracurricular activities. Once earned, these merits can never be taken away.

Today, a hundred percent of the students and staff—not to mention the parents themselves, who continued to play an important role—boast participation in this program. More than that, parents have taken to recognizing their children's achievements at home, both verbally and in writing. They rave about how their kids are more motivated to do well in school, more involved in extracurricular activities. And the parents communicate their sentiments in a variety of ways: at formal and informal conferences with the school staff, in customer service surveys, and so forth. In one instance, a student's uncle promised to salute her every time she earned higher ranking. Naturally the youngster set that as her goal, which helped her achieve it more rapidly.

IMPLEMENTATION

Implementing this particular school-wide acknowledgment program meant that as the students earned merits or points, they moved up in rank, earning in the course of the year certain privileges with each milestone. These privileges included certificates of advancement, special school-name badges and lanyards, daily front-of-the-lunch-line passes, celebration letters to parents from the principal, positive home visits by the principal, spirit items, field trips, privilege cards, commemorative plaques on the Wall of Fame, just to name a few.

In academics students received extra merits for scoring "Proficient" or "Advanced" on their common formative assessments. Should they subsequently fall short of that mark, they would still have the opportunity at a later date to retake the assessment exam. Not only did the superior score restore their merits, but it also became the official mark in their grade book. Thanks to this approach, students have come to enjoy myriad opportunities for demonstrating their mastery of grade-level standards.

Other ways to receive academic merits include Honor Roll and progress in electives. Plus, students can earn merits every two weeks for not being referred to the office for behavioral issues and for having perfect attendance. Last but not least, they can earn merits for extracurricular activities—sporting events, dances, after-school and weekend programs, parent nights, and so forth.

This type of school-wide Structure may appear simple in theory, but a detailed process requires lots of legwork and planning.

Action 1: Gather the staff together to discuss what is expected of the students. How should the students score on common assessments, district benchmarks, or any other tool? What behaviors are acceptable, which ones not? How about attendance, connecting the students to the school, and participation in extracurricular activities? Whatever happens, make sure your expectations are objective, quantifiable, and open to public scrutiny.

Action 2: Find easy, inexpensive privileges/rewards for students who meet expectations. These could be as simple as library, homework, or restroom passes; participation in a field day at the end of each semester; lunch in a special area of the campus; or choice on assignments. The possibilities being limitless, what really counts is that students have access to these privileges within an organized, systematic Structure.

Action 3: Put a doable plan in place. Resources (money, time, and staffing) should be allocated, responsibilities established, and specific actions initiated.

STRUCTURE STRATEGY 8: EMPLOY A LEARNING COMMUNITY SURVEY TO DRIVE SCHOOL-WIDE PRACTICES

Educators differ on how to assess implementation, and it is not unusual to find schools in the same district that use different tools. Here are some surveys conducted by leading authorities in this field:

- Huffman and Hipp (2003), in *Reculturing Schools as Professional Learning Communities*, analyze the Professional Learning Community Assessment (PLCA) based on a forty-five-question instrument to assess the perceptions of PLC principals and staff. In 2010, Olivier, Hipp, and Huffman improved on the survey by publishing the *Professional Learning Community Assessment—Revised (PLCA-R)*.
- Hord (1996) put out a seventeen-item School Professional Staff as Learning Community (SPSaLC) questionnaire, a useful gauge of staff perceptions about their school as a learning community.
- The PLC Continuum, created by DuFour et al. (2006), evaluates staff views on current PLC practices in schools. Participants decide the stages under which their school should fall (Pre-Initiation Stage, Initiation Stage, Developing Stage, and Sustaining Stage).

There are many other instruments. The one we use in our own schools is Huffman and Hipp's PLCA-R. Which instrument, if any, do you use to evaluate areas requiring attention in your PLC?

Here is one action we recommend.

Action 1: Start by reading the next chapter of this book, "The 4S Learning Community Assessment (4S-LCA)," to learn more about the instrument that can move every PLC strategy outlined in this book from theory to practice. This survey can be used as a stand-alone tool, or it can serve to support some other survey tool or framework already in place.

FIFTEEN
The 4S Learning Community Assessment (4S-LCA)

> A professional learning community is a group of individuals with common interests who share ideas and resources and support each other. It is fluid and comprises of people with different skill levels and on different journeys.
>
> —Anonymous teacher

We developed the 4S Learning Community Assessment (figure 15.1) to help PLCs assess staff's perceptions regarding thirty-two high-leverage strategies. This instrument will assist principals and teachers in determining which interventions can best improve the four quadrants named in our model: Standpoint, Struggle, Solidarity, and Structure.

The 4S Learning Community Assessment allows group members, in a sense, to make the invisible visible—presumably; as mortals we do not know what we don't know. In the following story, you will observe how a school, using the survey tool and action research, managed completely to transform its culture.

A STRUGGLE-ING SCHOOL

What a rollercoaster ride! The school had been bouncing back and forth in its annual test scores, as it tried to meet federal and state accountability measures. Some years it demonstrated significant growth, fulfilling each target it had set forth. But the scores dropped in other years, causing the school to miss its mark. The staff was terribly frustrated and about to call it a day.

The whole notion of a PLC, an initiative the school had decided to institute some years back, seemed less profitable than originally antici-

The 4S Learning Community Assessment

Directions: This instrument assesses your perceptions about the current reality of your school as it relates to a Professional Learning Community (PLC). Read each statement and then use the scale below to select the score that best reflects your personal degree of agreement with the statement. Be certain to select only one response for each statement. The "staff" represents all the employees at the school, including the principal, teachers, and other support employees. The "principal" represents the leader of the school.

Scale:
1 = Strongly Disagree   2 = Disagree   3 = Agree   4 = Strongly Agree

Quadrant #1: Standpoint	1	2	3	4
1. The staff regularly extends their trust to help build positive relationships with one another.				
2. The staff readily knows the strengths of other staff members.				
3. The staff regularly uses effective meeting designs.				
4. The staff regularly takes the time to *walk in others' shoes*.				
5. The staff regularly celebrates the diversity of the PLC.				
6. The staff regularly reflects on their own perspectives and how other may react.				
7. The staff and the principal have a positive, constructive relationship.				
8. The staff understands the political history of the school and community.				

Quadrant #2: Struggle	1	2	3	4
9. The staff practices honest and transparent, even through the difficult conversations.				
10. The staff regularly balances task and relationship when carrying out different responsibilities.				
11. The staff has explicitly developed school-wide agreements to deal with unhealthy conflict.				
12. The staff's actions are in alignment with the school's overarching mission and vision.				
13. The staff regularly focuses on the problem, and not the individual, when disagreement occurs.				
14. The staff successfully works through differences to solve problems.				
15. The staff regularly seeks agreement and communicates reasoning behind decisions.				
16. The staff regularly apologizes meaningfully, communicating that relationships are important.				

Quadrant #3: Solidarity	1	2	3	4
17. The staff accepts different ways of accomplishing tasks, and encourages risk taking.				
18. The staff has collaboratively developed team agreements that further support school-wide agreements.				
19. The staff supports greater good, rather than individual interests.				
20. The staff regularly attends to group maintenance and processes.				
21. The staff uses a team survey instrument to help develop teamwork and unity.				
22. The staff incorporates individual goals and passions into the organizational mission and vision.				
23. The staff regularly celebrates personal and professional successes.				
24. The staff regularly enjoys food and play together.				

Quadrant #4: Structure	1	2	3	4
25. The staff has designed time, location, and opportunity for collaboration.				
26. The staff has autonomy in delivering instruction, interventions, and enrichment.				
27. The staff regularly takes an action research approach.				
28. The staff conducts site based professional development.				
29. The staff has a systematic tiered intervention system.				
30. The staff uses common formative assessments to monitor student learning and drive practices.				
31. The staff has a school-wide acknowledgement system for students.				
32. The staff uses a learning community survey to drive school-wide practices.				

Figure 15.1. The 4S Learning Community Assessment (4S-LCA)

pated. Yet the staff could not find fault in any of the systems. The teachers were organized mainly into PLC-type teams. With ample time for regular meetings, many of them had managed to develop common formative assessments, and tiered interventions were not uncommon.

So why the erratic results?

Sadly, this school operated only in the third and fourth quadrants (in reference to the Knowledge/Success Matrix of our last chapter). This explained why it was sometimes "successful," and why staff had no idea what had led to success or failure. Such ambiguity bothered the staff, so they decided to investigate the 4S Approach using the 4S-LCA as a catalyst.

First, they met to Frame the situation at hand.

FRAMING QUADRANT 1: STANDPOINT

This is the district's most seasoned staff. There are very few "green" teachers, and the average tenure is around thirteen years. Moreover, many members have traditionally been vocal in sharing their perspectives. The principal has encouraged this, thanks to his penchant for collaboration. By and large, everyone appreciated the opportunities for input on decisions affecting everyone. Some staff meetings brought everyone together to search for solutions to complex issues as they arose. Others became venues for sharing general information about current topics. It was a bit like hit-and-miss.

To add to their predicament, a couple of members appeared not to value or even acknowledge the viewpoints of their colleagues—a few rotten apples spoiling the rest.

FRAMING QUADRANT 2: STRUGGLE

Standpoint may not necessarily be a major issue, but the school's conflicts stemmed from deep-seated differences in views. Yelling matches among some teachers have already broken out in the halls and staff lounge. In a couple of instances e-mail exchanges were misconstrued, which lead to even more discord.

Is this their way of refusing to work with peers? If so, they are doing a good job. The squabbles have so damaged relationships that not even the staff wanted to work together. Their Struggle made that too difficult.

FRAMING QUADRANT 3: SOLIDARITY

Campus teams function at high levels when camaraderie is in evidence and tasks are being completed more or less efficiently. On the other hand, their failure to see eye-to-eye on important matters, should it come to that, has ignited a destructive Struggle and taxed the patience of every member, some of whom have drifted to a more comfortable space—isolation.

FRAMING QUADRANT 4: STRUCTURE

The school enjoys great systems, but some teachers still found it difficult to work collaboratively within them. No wonder the test scores differed so widely from year to year. Staff and faculty have been going through the motions and little else. After much discussion and debate, the staff concluded,

> The right systems are visibly present. However, the letdown in results has essentially been the result of the staff's failure to regularly acknowledge—and prevail over—the natural conflict that goes together with different points of view. And as a result, collaboration is meager at best.

It was time to "Assess." The status quo not being an option, no matter how comfortable it may seem, the members considered the 4S-LCA survey tool, which they believed may help them improve their capacity for collaboration.

The survey results were telling about the school and the members of the PLC. The statistical means were calculated from data touching on each of the 4S-LCA questions. Below were the items with the highest means:

- *Question #32:* The staff uses a learning community survey to drive school-wide practices (mean of 3.36).
- *Question #25:* The staff designs time, location, and opportunity for collaboration (mean of 3.32).
- *Question #8*: The staff understands the political history of the school and community (mean of 3.24).

Overall, the quadrants for Standpoint and Structure (both with means of 3.05) showed the highest means compared to the other end of the spectrum.

The survey also measured the following staff perceptions, which were the lowest item means:

- *Question #11*: The staff has developed explicit school-wide agreements to deal with unhealthy conflict (mean of 1.80).
- *Question #14:* The staff successfully works through differences to solve problems (mean of 2.44).
- *Question #20:* The staff regularly attends to group maintenance and processes (mean of 2.60).

At the same time, Struggle—the second quadrant—showed the lowest mean by a wide margin. Clearly, this was a Struggle-ing school.

Armed with these data, staff was in a better position to "Diagnose" the problems, identifying what may have led to low scores in some areas. First, though, they decided to celebrate the high-scoring areas.

The question with the highest mean—namely, *staff use of a learning community survey to drive school-wide practices*—resulted from the members adopting the 4S-LCA. This bold step allowed staff to take the temperature of the school, while openly and honestly scrutinizing its own school-wide behaviors and practices. It was a great place to start.

The question with the second highest mean—*designing time, location, and opportunity for collaboration*—often constitutes the biggest barrier for schools, but not this school, which benefited from allocating enough time for all the members to discover new practices and tweak current ones.

Question #8, regarding *the staff's understanding of the political history of the school and community*, likely issued from staff experience. With an average tenure of around thirteen years, most of members feel they understand the school's traditions and where it has been.

After celebrating the areas with high mean figures, the staff members put their heads together and identified why some areas had not scored so well. For example, Question #11, regarding *staff's development of explicit school-wide agreements to deal with unhealthy conflict*, scored significantly lower than all other items, the most typical responses being "Strongly Disagree" and "Disagree." The truth is that the members have yet to gather formally and hash out norms or agreements, which omission of has led to unhealthy Struggle, ineffective processes, reduced communication, and poor working relationships.

With no road map outlining expected behaviors, the staff had great trouble working through their differences (Question #14). Question #20—regarding *staff regularly attending to group maintenance and processes*—showed a low score for the same reason: principals and teachers normally find it difficult just to sit together to talk about their follow-throughs, or lack thereof, as they relate to behavior and practice.

Once the problems became crystal clear, however, it was time for "Planning and Action." To ensure the plan was manageable, the school's Leadership Team came together and developed S.M.A.R.T. goals (Specific, Measurable, Attainable, Results-Oriented, and Timely), a term popularized by DuFour et al.'s (2006) work on PLCs.

Figure 15.2 displays their completed S.M.A.R.T. goal worksheet. It consists of five columns—goal, specific steps, responsibility, timeline, and evidence of effectiveness.

Situation in Need of Attention (SITNA): 4S-LCA #1 – *Struggle & Solidarity*		School *Struggle*-ing School		Date: xx/xx/xxxx
Data & Goal	**Steps/Strategies**	**Responsibility**	**Timeline**	**Evidence of Effectiveness**
1. The areas on the 4S-LCA #1 with the two lowest means were, *The staff has explicitly developed school-wide agreements to deal with unhealthy conflict* (1.80), and, *The staff successfully works through differences to solve problems* (2.44).	1. The staff will, over the course of two professional development meetings, collectively develop—and agree upon—productive school norms concerning staff behaviors, communication, and decision-making. Much emphasis will be placed on behaviors for working through differences.	1. The professional development team will seek, from a variety of resources, fitting meeting designs for collective agreement development. The team will also develop the meeting agendas and logistics.	1. The professional development team will meet next week to plan the meeting activities that will happen during the last two meetings this month.	Quantitative data from the 4S-LCA #2, as well as other informal and formal feedback from members of the school, will be used to determine success of both interventions. Note. The 4S-LCA #2 will be conducted again in three months.
2. The area on the 4S-LCA #1 with the third lowest mean was, *The staff regularly attends to group maintenance and processes* (2.60).	2. The whole staff and teams will take a monthly "time-out" to evaluate the school's processes, behaviors, and follow through with all established agreements. Agreements will be refined if necessary.	2. The principal and professional development team will explicitly include regular "time-outs" in the master calendar, which is sent out to the staff each month.	2. Next month's master calendar will visibly include time for these "time-outs."	
Goal: Following a sequence of activities, the expected outcome is for each of the above-mentioned areas to score a mean above 3.0 on the 4S-LCA #2.				

Figure 15.2. S.M.A.R.T. Goal Worksheet

The team felt that two simple, high-leverage strategies would get the PLC moving in the right direction. Simply put, if they were serious about collaboration, then staff had to agree on what their group effort ought to look like.

Here are the strategies they employed:

- **Strategy #1:** Staff will, over the course of two professional development meetings, collectively develop—and agree upon—productive school norms concerning staff behavior, communication, and decision making. Emphasis will be placed on behaviors for working through differences.
- **Strategy #2:** Staff and teams will take a monthly time-out to evaluate the school's processes, behaviors, and follow through with any established agreements. Agreements will be refined if necessary.

Their ambition, outlined in table 15.1, was to earn a mean score above 3.0 for questions 11, 14, and 20 when the 4S-LCA was conducted the second time three months down the road.

With both strategies coming into place everything else began to gel. The damaging interactions between members began to diminish. Those staff members who had found it impossible to work together even in the best of times drew closer as new ideas began to surface. Everyone worked effectively and efficiently within the Structure, confident that the test scores would climb. The school's personality shifted, accordingly, toward the notion that *we are smarter than me!*

A few months later the second round of the 4S-LCA was conducted. The school flourished; practices were really at their best. Happily, the items that had first yielded the lowest means increased significantly this time around.

The staff seemed to have met their goal. Yet this time, as expected, new items yielded low statistical means, which was fine since—as mentioned in the last chapter—change always occurred in loops.

So Frame, Assess, Diagnose, Plan, then Repeat.

SIXTEEN
You're Hired!

> A professional learning community is a group of educators who join together with the goal of improving instruction and learning for students. The individuals are committed to conducting research and examining best teaching practices in the classroom. Once they have identified the educational focus for the group they examine books and research material, visit other school districts, observe in classrooms, prepare teaching lessons, conduct demonstration lessons for the group and evaluate the effectiveness of the lessons. Once they have determined what works best for their student population they develop curriculum and materials that reinforce the techniques developed for their students. It is an extremely effective tool for improving student learning and supporting a core of professionals who are devoted to improving their classroom instruction.
> —Mary Mascher, state legislator and former teacher, Des Moines, IA

The interviewee we presented in our very first chapter best expressed how the final question ought to be treated. After some pause—*click, clock, click, clock*—the words rolled off his tongue in a tone more serious than on any previous question: "Our district is focusing on professional learning communities. Please thoroughly share with us your definition and understanding of a professional learning community, as well as how you would bring one into practice."

The candidate for the job paused to collect her own thoughts and to consider all she has learned and experienced with PLCs. "The term *PLC* is made up of three distinct words: *professional, learning, community*. Understanding a PLC brings focus on both its development and path."

The gentleman asks, "Could you explain that for us."

"Well, if an administrator focuses on *professional*, then he or she should be able to make tangible changes for the PLC. This person gives staff and faculty official time and space to meet. But if we just expect everyone to be 'professional,' there really is no nurturing of member relationships. Members are simply being told when and where to meet but never how to meet. There is an investment in time but not much else. Decisions are made; things get done, yet the members never really come together."

She went on, "The same goes for the word *learning*. What happens here is that the PLC focuses exclusively on student learning, rather than member learning. It's funny, because schools say they value lifelong learning but never really practice it. Again, member relationships are not nurtured and team unity is merely assumed." She pauses. "But when a PLC focuses on *community*, things are different."

"Different? How so?" asks the gentleman.

"When the focus is on *community*, the PLC learns to grow by means of its greatest resource: the members and their interconnections with one another. Each PLC has its own culture, and it is the members who create and maintain that culture. From the culture comes the commitment to cooperate and collaborate. Therefore, it only makes sense to develop the PLC's strength through its members' diversity, conflict, teamwork, and organizational structure."

Our 4S Approach privileges individuality but in a cooperative mode that keeps within the PLC model. In the past, the development of PLCs focused too narrowly on formal Structure and curriculum delivery and assessment. Without diminishing the value of either of these two components, member relationships occupy a greater place in the health and success of the PLC. They can build the culture of cooperation and collaboration necessary to achieve *true* PLC status.

The membership has to find recognition and be valued. After that anything is possible, though shaping and adhering to the school's norms, policies, and goals can only come from the members who buy into them. The success of every student intervention program rests on the contributions of the PLC members, just as the creation and implementation of innovative solutions to site-specific problems come from the collective wisdom and will of the PLC members.

All members must work to develop the culture of school and learning community.

Don't sit back expecting a few bell-schedule changes and meeting times to bring about the desired change. Take an honest look at your organization. Reflect on its strengths and opportunities for growth.

Our 4S Approach will empower your PLC to leave its mark as an educational institution, perhaps as a model for others to follow.

Bibliography

Ainsworth, L., & Viegut, D. (2006). *Common formative assessments: How to connect standards-based instruction and assessment*. Thousand Oaks, CA: Corwin Press.

Arroyo, H. (2011). *Strategies used by successful professional learning communities to maintain Hord's dimensions of PLCs and include new members*. Ed.D. dissertation, University of La Verne.

Bailey, K., & Jakicic, C. (2012). *Common formative assessments: A toolkit for professional learning communities*. Bloomington, IN: Solution Tree.

Bunker, B., & Alban, B. (2006). *The handbook of large group methods: Creating systemic change in organizations and communities*. San Francisco, CA: Jossey-Bass.

Delisio, E., (2009). Organizing staff meetings even you want to attend. Education World. Retrieved from www.educationworld.com/a_admin/admin/admin518.shtml, January 2010.

DuFour, R. (1998). *Professional learning communities at work: Best practices for enhancing student achievement*. Bloomington, IN: Solution Tree.

DuFour, R. (2008). *Revisiting professional learning communities at work: New insights for improving schools*. Bloomington, IN: Solution Tree.

DuFour, R. P., DuFour, R. B., & Eaker, R. (eds.). (2005). *On common ground: The power of professional learning communities*. Bloomington, IN: Solution Tree.

DuFour, R., DuFour, R., Eaker, R., & Karhanek, G. (2004). *Whatever it takes: How professional learning communities respond when kids don't learn*. Bloomington, IN: Solution Tree.

DuFour, R. P., DuFour, R. B., Eaker, R., & Many, T. (2006). *Learning by doing: A handbook for professional learning communities at work*. Bloomington, IN: Solution Tree.

Fullan, M. (1991). *The new meaning of educational change*. New York: Teachers College Press.

Fullan, M. G., & Miles, M. B. (1992). Getting reform right: What works and what doesn't. *Phi Delta Kappan* 73, 745–52.

Harvey, T. (2009). *Toward collaboration in district/association relationships: ABC School District*. Educational Policy Institute of California (EPIC). University of La Verne.

Harvey, T., Bearley, W., & Corkrum, S. (2001). *The practical decision maker*. Lanham, MD: Scarecrow Education.

Harvey, T., & Drolet, B. (2004). *Building teams, building people: Expanding the fifth resource*. Lanham, MD: Scarecrow Education.

Heifetz, R., & Linsky, M. (2002). *Leadership on the line: Staying alive through the dangers of leading*. Boston: Harvard Business School Press.

Holman, P., Devane, T., & Cady, S. (2007). *The change handbook: The definitive resource on today's best methods for engaging whole systems*. San Francisco, CA: Berrett-Koehler.

Hord, S. (1987). *Evaluating educational innovation*. New South Wales: Croom Helm.

Hord, S. (1996). *School professional staff as learning community questionnaire*. Austin: Southwest Educational Development Laboratory.

Hord, S. M. (1997). Professional learning communities: What are they and why are they important? *Issues about Change*, 6(1), 1–8.

Hord, S. (2004). *Learning together, leading together*. New York: Southwest Educational Development Laboratory.

Hord, S., Meehan, M., Orletsky, S., & Sattes, B. (1999). Assessing a school staff as a community of professional learners. *Issues about Change* 7(1).

Huffman, J., & Hipp, K. (2003). *Reculturing schools as professional learning communities.* Lanham, MD: Scarecrow Education.

Jehn, K., (1995). A multimethod examination of the benefits and detriments of intragroup conflict. *Administrative Science Quarterly* 40, 256–282.

Joiner, B., & Josephs, S. (2007). *Leadership agility: Five levels of mastery for anticipating and initiating change.* San Francisco, CA: Jossey-Bass.

Jones, J., & Bearley, W. (2001). Facilitating team development: A view from the field. *Group Facilitation: A Research and Applications Journal* 3, 56–65.

King, E., Hebl, M., & Beal, D. (2009). Conflict and cooperation in diverse workgroups. *Journal of Social Issues* 65(2), 261–285.

Levi, D. (2001). *Group dynamics of teams.* Thousand Oaks, CA: Sage Publications.

Libert, B., & Spector, J. (2008). *We are smarter than me: How to unleash the power of crowds in your business.* Upper Saddle River, NJ: Pearson Education.

Marzano, R. (2005). *School leadership that works: From research to results.* Alexandria, VA: Association for Supervision and Curriculum Development.

Marzano, R. (2006). *Classroom assessment and grading that work.* Alexandria, VA: ASCD.

McLaughlin, M., & Talbert, J. (2001). *Professional communities and the work of high school teaching.* Chicago, IL: University of Chicago Press.

Morr, S. (2010). *The dynamics of team characteristics within professional learning communities.* Ed.D. dissertation, University of La Verne.

Muhammad, A. (2009). *Transforming school culture: Overcoming staff division.* Bloomington, IN: Solution Tree Press.

Nelson, T. (2009). Teacher's collaborative inquiry and professional growth: Should we be optimistic? *Science Education* 93(3), 548–580.

Northcraft, G., Polzer, J., Neale, M., & Kramer, R. (1995). Productivity in cross functional teams: Diversity, social identity and performance. Washington, DC: APA Publications, 69–96.

Olivier, D. F., Hipp, K. K., and Huffman, J.B. (2010). *Demystifying professional learning communities: School leadership at its best.* Lanham, MD: Rowman & Littlefield Education.

Oshry, B., (2007). *Seeing systems: Unlocking the mysteries of organizational life.* San Francisco, CA: Berrett-Koehler Publishers.

Patterson, K., Grenny, J., McMillan, R., & Switzler, A. (2004). *Crucial confrontations: Tools for resolving broken promises, violated expectations, and bad behavior.* New York: McGraw-Hill.

Random House. (2001). *Random House Webster's Dictionary*, revised edition. New York: Random House.

Richter, N. (2012). *Effective teams: The four key foundations as a framework for understanding school success.* Ed.D. dissertation, University of La Verne.

Rosenberg, M. (2003). *Nonviolent communication: A language of life.* Encinitas, CA: PuddleDancer Press.

Rosenholtz, S. (1989). *Teacher's workplace: The social organization of schools.* New York: Teachers College Press.

Ryan, M. (2003). *The power of patience.* New York: Broadway Books.

Sawyer, J. Houlette, M., & Yeagley, E. (2006). Decision performance and diversity structure: Comparing faultiness in divergent, crosscut, and facially homogeneous groups. *Organizational Behavior and Decision Processes* 99, 1–15.

Schmoker, M. (2004). Tipping point: From feckless reform to substantive instructional improvement. *Phi Delta Kappan* 85(6), 424–432.

Schmoker, M. (2006). *Results now: How we can achieve unprecedented improvements in teaching and learning.* Alexandria, VA: ASCD.

Senge, P. (1990). *The fifth discipline: The art and practice of the learning organization.* New York: Currency Doubleday.

Southwest Educational Development Laboratory. (1997). Professional learning communities: What are they and why are they important? *Issues about Change* 6(1), 1.

Thompson, G., & Jenkins, J. (2004). *Verbal judo: The gentle art of persuasion*. New York: HarperCollins.

Ulrich, D. (1996). *Credibility x capability*. In F. Hesselbein, M. Goldsmith, & R. Beckhard (eds.), *The leader of the future* (pp. 209–220). San Francisco: Jossey-Bass.

Von Oech, R. (2006). *Creative whack pack*. New York: Warner Books.

Weeks, D. (1994). *The eight essential steps in conflict resolution: Preserving relationships at work, at home and in the community*. New York: Penguin Putnam.

Wiseman, P. (2008). *Professional learning communities and the effectiveness of the teams within those communities*. Ed.D. dissertation, University of La Verne.

Wiseman, P. (2010). *Strong schools, strong leaders: What matters most in times of change*. Lanham, MD: Rowman & Littlefield Publishers.

Wiseman, P., & Arroyo, H. (2011). *Professional learning communities and their impact on student achievement*. Educational Policy Institute of California (EPIC). University of La Verne.

About the Authors

Perry Wiseman is currently the director of Student Programs for the Los Angeles County Office of Education, working closely with principals and teachers reaching at-risk students who fall through the cracks in the public educational system. He is former school principal, founder of the educational consulting firm WiseFoundations (www.wisefoundations.com), and author of the book *Strong Schools, Strong Leaders*. He is an energetic educator recognized for his collaborative manner and instructional innovation.

Perry has a true commitment to the learning and development of others. His enthusiasm and vigor make each shared venture a memorable one. He holds a doctorate in organizational leadership from the University of La Verne and a master's degree in educational administration from the University of Redlands.

Hector Arroyo works at Western University Health Sciences in Pomona as a learning skills specialist. In this position he collaborates with administration, faculty, and mentors to help graduate students overcome the challenges of medical school. He has ten years of experience teaching English at the middle and high school levels. He also taught various general education courses, including composition, research methods, and group dynamics for five years as an adjunct instructor at a local technical college.

Hector holds a bachelor's degree in English, a master's degree in education, and a doctoral degree in organizational leadership.

Nicholas Richter is a high school principal with thirteen years of experience in education. He started his educational career as a high school mathematics teacher. Nick successfully found ways to relate a difficult subject to students and even had a little fun doing it. Nick worked for six years as an assistant principal at comprehensive high schools. After that, Nick took his first principalship as a continuation principal. Then he took a position as a comprehensive high school principal. This wide array of educational experiences provides a practitioner's perspective to the strategies in this book.

Nick holds two majors on his bachelor's degree, mathematics and Spanish, a master's degree in educational management, and a doctorate in organizational leadership. More than anything, Nick is a tirelessly dedicated educator who has spent his career improving learning for all students. He lives by the simple motto, "Ensure all students learn."

www.ingramcontent.com/pod-product-compliance
Lightning Source LLC
Chambersburg PA
CBHW061841300426
44115CB00013B/2467